Addictions Counseling:

Introduction to Theory and Practice

By: Stan E. DeKoven, Ph.D.

Addictions Counseling:

Introduction to Theory and Practice

ISBN#: 1-931178-65-8

Vision Publishing
1520 Main Street, Suite C
Ramona CA 92065
www.visionpublishingservices.com

Second Edition 2004
Printed In The United States Of America

All scripture references are taken from the New King James Version of the Bible unless otherwise noted.

Disclaimer

Any case studies presented in this book are real. The names and circumstances however, have been altered to protect the privacy of the individuals involved. The information in this text is intended for use by professional counselors, pastoral counselors and related helping professions or training programs within those fields.

It is not intended as a manual for "self help" or self treatment of personal addiction problems of an individual. Addictive and abusive substance problems must be treated under the guidance and supervision of duly licensed or trained individuals.

Those who are addicted to chemical substances or suspect that they may be, are strongly recommended to obtain the assistance of a professionally trained substance addiction counselor or other licensed professional.

Table of Contents

Dedication

This book is dedicated to those who fight the battle for freedom from the abusive and destructive affects of chemical addiction.

Preface

In this book we are going to cover the most important aspects of counseling effectively with people that are suffering from substance addiction. Further, we are going to look at many of the controversial issues and treatment models that go along with substance abuse: the disease model, versus the sin model, versus the social model.

Some important statistics falling under the heading of etiology (the science which describes how diseases begin) are worth consideration. The latest statistics indicate that 87% of all Americans are raised in a dysfunctional family. Thus, a very significant amount of the American population have suffered from some sort of severe psycho-social trauma in their upbringing. People do not want to admit these problems. They include divorce, abuse of various kinds, being raised in an alcoholic or drug addicted family system or being raised in a family where one or both parents were mentally ill.

These life circumstances can cause a great deal of difficulty for people. Even if the parents were not alcoholics, if personal primary needs were not met, any person can fit into the category of being dysfunctional. One primary manifestation of this pattern of dysfunctional family interaction is the increase of alcoholism and drug addiction. There is probably not a family in America that is not immediately impacted by the abuse of or addiction to drugs and alcohol. We all know people that have been or are presently addicted to some type of substance or compulsive behavioral patterns that enables them to "survive" life. However, these learned dysfunctional behaviors do not help any of them to function adequately in life as a whole.

Almost all families have at least one member usually hidden "in the closet:" a homosexual, drug addict, alcoholic, habitual criminal behavior, etc. To achieve a better understanding of this dynamic of disease in family life, the natural mind, family dynamics and the psycho-social medical models of substance abuse along with their treatments will be presented. Further, the text investigates the scriptural revelation on substance addiction and abuse, co-dependency as well as provides a broadened theological framework for treatment and ministry to the abuser and the family.

9

Substance abuse is but one of many forms of compulsive behavior where people attempt to meet legitimate needs in illegitimate ways. Our responsibility as spiritual leaders in a world of physical pain is to minister God's grace and mercy with knowledge and understanding to the wounded, especially for those caught in the destructive pattern of alcohol or drug abuse.

We desire to fully acknowledge all of those individuals who though having a desire for privacy contributed to the stories and backgrounds forming the motivation for this work.

We firstly want to acknowledge the many students of Vision University for their commitment to pursue this very critical and difficult area of study in preparation for forming their own part in the healing of those who are hurting.

We further want to acknowledge the families of both Dr. DeKoven and Rev. King for their encouragement along the way in this ongoing work.

Most of all, we want to acknowledge our Lord and Savior, Jesus Christ *"who would have all men be saved,"* and having saved them, now desires that they become and eternally remain free from every, *"yoke of bondage."*

"Stand fast therefore in the liberty with which Christ has made us free," (Galatians 5:1).

For ease of usage, terms commonly understood by professionals but not as commonly with non-professionals but not as commonly with non-professionals have a member by it, which is keyed to Defined/Terms in the back of the book. Though the book was written for the average reader, some usage of clinical terms are inevitable this defined.

Dr. Stan DeKoven

Acknowledgements

My special thanks to all of those individuals who, though having a desire for privacy, contributed to the stories and backgrounds forming the motivation for this work.

I further acknowledge the many students of Vision International University for their commitment to pursue this very critical and difficult area of study, in preparation for forming their own part in the healing of those who are hurting.

I also want to acknowledge and than the DeKoven family for their encouragement along the way in this ongoing work.

Most of all, acknowledge belongs to the Lord and Savior, Jesus Christ, *"who would have all men be saved,"* and having saved them, now desires that they become and remain, eternally, free from every *"yoke of bondage"*.

"Stand fast therefore in the liberty by which Christ has made us free, and do not be entangled again with a yoke of bondage," (Galatians 5:1).

Part 1

Substance Abuse Therapy

Chapter One

What is Substance Abuse?

Most physicians and psychiatrists classify substance abuse as a disease or medical disorder. The real question is: what is the source of this disease? Is it genetically ingrained into certain individuals, or do drugs and alcohol propagate the disease? It is much like the question of old, "Which came first, the chicken or the egg."

There are inconclusive studies on both sides!

In order to see the full picture we must first look at the spiritual side of this malady. In the scriptures, drugs come under the concept of "pharmacia" which were used in the enhancement of prayer during religious ceremonies and witchcraft. This type of activity is clearly forbidden in the Word of God.

As it relates to alcohol, there is the proper use and abuse of it as described in the Word. However, despite concepts of scriptural tolerance, wisdom must be used and personal choices made when it comes to this powerful substance. For those who are bound by alcohol, *abstinence*[1] is generally seen as the best course for life.

Let's take a brief look at the importance of a good diagnosis. Without a good diagnosis you cannot develop a good treatment plan. Any trained or licensed physician would assert, "Triage has to occur first. You've got to know where to put the patient. You've got to know what the problem is before you apply treatment strategies and you always deal with the most critical things first and move on from there therapeutically."

Unmet Needs: A Basic Foundation For Addiction?

We all know instinctively that there are needs that all humans have in common. These would include food, air, clothing, shelter, a sense of safety, purpose and relationship. These cover the physical and logical needs of survival. There are also primary emotional needs which must be met and should be supplied within family life, which are the keys to wholeness or brokeness.

---

[1] Words in **Bold** and *Italics* are defined at the end of the book.

The **first primary emotional need** for all people is the innate need for love. Everyone is looking for love: a sense of being wanted, needed, desired, etc. In a functional family, love is experienced on a regular and consistent basis in a multitude of ways. This love would be experienced as acceptance, warmth, being touched, held, hugged and nurtured. In a *dysfunctional* family, love is not experienced at all, or, at a minimum, provided on an inconsistent basis for the individual. When love is not experienced, emotional pain is the result. To anesthetize that pain, people tend to substitute various activities for the missing love. This is done automatically and unconsciously.

The choices made are dependent upon a number of factors, which include genetics, the environment one is raised in, peer pressure, as well as a host of others. Whether one will choose drugs, alcohol, sexual misbehavior, eating or other *compulsive* behaviors is entirely dependent upon the individual in question.

The **second primary need** is for security. Security is experienced in a functional family as protection (not over-protection) mixed with direction or guidance from the primary caregivers (parents). In a dysfunctional family there is a lack of protection or a feeling of smothering. Another word we might use is *enmeshment*. A real problem in modern culture today is neglect. Neglect occurs where a child is allowed to completely make his/her own decisions without parental consent or control. This may feel good to the child and ultimately to the adolescent, but it is not healthy. Children left to make all of their own decisions rarely make good ones, no matter how well wired they may be. Even when they do make good choices, they generally grow up with resentment and bitterness having not received the guidance that they really needed.

A **third primary need** is worth or esteem. Worth in a functional family requires the freedom to be and the freedom to do, mixed with honesty. Relationships that are honest and open create a sense that one has value, a sense that "I am worth something." Akin to that is the experience of forgiveness. All children do things wrong. Parents should live in a state that forgiveness is readily given without condemnation. In a dysfunctional family there is a lack of a healthy self worth. In fact, these families propagate worthlessness through manipulation on the part of the parents. The manipulation is exhibited through the conditional love exercised by the parents, who attempt to mold children into the parent's image. This alone creates a lack of worth in a child.

The **fourth primary emotional need** is protection. This need is closely related to security. Protection instinctively says that if one is in danger the family will be there to give support. Security speaks of a solid foundation. Protection is "If I've stepped outside of the family, I do not risk the loss of family. I know that my family will be there through thick or thin." In a dysfunctional family, however at best, there is a limited experience of protection. In this family system everybody is more or less on their own. However, there is one cardinal rule which binds a dysfunctional family together. It says "don't bring any embarrassment to the family." Shame, and its accompanying emotion: fear, are the bonds which hold a Dysfunctional *family system* together.

The **fifth primary emotional need** is the need for provision. This is the need to be provided for physically, emotionally, spiritually, and financially. In functional families, these key needs are provided for regularly, consistently, and to the best of that family's ability. In a healthy family, provision is seen as the vital part of being a family.

Statements typifying such a family system would be, "Of course, we will provide for you the best that we can because we are family." In a dysfunctional family, there will be a lack of consistent provision due to the acting out behaviors of the parents or the other dysfunctional aspects of the overall family structure. Even when there is apparently an ample provision made for the children, in a corrupt family system it is done so with excessive and conflicting requirements or strings attached.

These Needs At Work In The Family

In the DeKoven family, my parents had very few emotional strings in terms of what they would give or what they would withhold. My father doesn't believe in giving money, he believes in loaning money, and wants to be paid back. But in the generation before his, with my grandmother and her two sisters, (we affectionately called them the wig sisters because they wore so many different wigs they couldn't keep them on straight) they would use their money to control and manipulate the family. They were able to give and did give, but they always wanted something in return that obligated the family members to them. This manipulation made it difficult to develop any real sense of closeness with them.

Both methods of provision can be, and are frequently, quite destructive. No provision, or support contingent on repayment says, "I will support you as LOVE would dictate in the short term, as long as it costs me nothing in the long term." And frequently it means, "My selfish desires must not be impacted by your legitimate needs. You are not important to me."

Provision offered with "strings" attached can be good if they relate to learning the responsible use of resources and <u>deadly</u> when they are self-serving and manipulative. One friend of ours in ministry today was blackmailed into a marital relationship at a very premature age which resulted in a hostile divorce over a decade later. The trauma that this tragedy produced has landed several of the children in the hospital (for drug overdose) or in jail (public misbehavior) a multitude of times. What a tragedy!

"Strings" attached to provision can put people in careers of fields of study not of their own choosing, perpetuating a lifestyle choice of perpetual misery. There is an overall sense of "I must not be lovable as I am to deserve support. I must become what I am not in order to be loved..." perhaps the first of many masks an addict learns to wear.

In a functional family the environment is filled with love and acceptance, forgiveness, protection, honesty, freedom (in proper measure). Generally, the parents are truth seekers, seeking the best for one another. In a dysfunctional family, there is some form of addictive or other ***obsessive compulsive behavior*** such as substance abuse, eating disorders or sexual acting out. Often, there is divorce or abuse within the family system. What is experienced in this home is condemnation, manipulation, neglect, denial and a lack of honesty in relationships. This is certainly not what God intended, nor is it where God intends for us to remain or perpetuate.

The result of a functional family is a balanced life; physically, socially, mentally, and spiritually. In Luke 2:52, talking about Jesus' life we read;

> *"And Jesus increased in wisdom and stature, and in favor with God and men."*

Wisdom speaks of our intellectual and spirit man. As Jesus grew in His spirit and intellectually, so must we. Thus, our intellectual and spiritual life is to be nurtured in family life. Stature speaks to our physical life, which also needs nurturing or affirmation. Affirming that we are created in the likeness of God. Favor speaks to our purpose, towards God to worship Him and grow in relationship to the Father, affirming the image of God and our dominion through Him. And, finally, with men speaks of our relationship with man. Jesus spoke of this in its ultimate form in Luke

10:25-27,

> *"And behold, a certain lawyer stood up and tested Him, saying, 'Teacher, what shall I do to inherit eternal life?' He said to him, 'What is written in the law? What is your reading of it?' So he answered and said, 'You shall love the LORD your God with all your heart, with all your soul, with all your strength, and with all your mind, and your neighbor as yourself.'"*

In a functional family system there is balance leading to growth. Nobody is perfect, nor is it expected, but we must maintain balance. This is where relational health lies. There seems to be a "give" and "take" in healthy relationships along with mutual respect. In a healthy family system love can be freely expressed, along with anger, fear, and laughter. All emotions are acceptable depending upon the context of the particular situation. There is an intimacy within that family. When the family members talk about one another there is a glimmer of joy, hope and grace in their eye. My word and deed, it is apparent they really do care for one another.

It is wonderful to see that healthy dynamics can also be observed in functional church families. When its members talk about their church, they do so with a bubbly "little kid" kind of feeling or a sense of pride, love, appreciation and a genuine affection toward other members of their fellowship. This sign of intimacy is one indication of a healthy growing church. Proper **boundaries** are another profound indicator. There is room for individual difference and personal liberty within the overall goals of family life. A functional Church family like can be a powerful model for those raised in a dysfunctional family system. It can be a substitute or surrogate family that fills the deficiencies of love, acceptance and support. Even to the dysfunctionally loud person, there is hope in God's family, His Church!

Another dynamic of healthy family life is a willingness to engage life to its fullest. The focus of family life is to grow, to become, and to change. Though there is a certain amount of anxiety about growth and change in all families, the healthy family has common goals, beliefs and desires that all share. Each individual within this system knows where he or the others are headed. We all know there is no perfect family, but many are working on becoming their best. This is hope.

In a dysfunctional family, **co-dependent** and triangular relationships exist which lack truth or the ability to fully see truth. In other words, they become blinded because of the environment they were raised in. Co-dependents are people who often have an acute sense of responsibility that is warped in one way or another. (More on co-dependency later).

Functional families remain balanced with little or no **triangulation**. They share responsibilities and can divide the needs and responsibilities among one another. They basically know "what's my responsibility," from "what's yours."

Dysfunctional families respond to life in the extreme. Some families will have members who are totally irresponsible contrasted to those that are totally responsible. Usually in such families, the totally responsible person would be the "co-dependent." The totally irresponsible person would typically be "the addict" or one "with compulsive behavior."

Whether they are actually using substances or something else is irrelevant. The addict is acting irresponsible. They do what they feel, what they want, whenever they want to, without regard for other people's needs or feelings. The spouse or child who is not the addict takes total responsibility for the addict's irresponsibility, creating a codependent dance. This can be seen in any dysfunctional family and in every alcoholic, drug abusing family system. Further, there is a controlling cycle. Co-dependents vacillate between, "I want to be controlled" to "I want to be completely out of control." Back and forth it goes; nothing is in balance for long. They are totally double-minded people, unstable in all their ways (James). The codependent is actually addicted to the family imbalance! There is usually significant guilt, hurt, anger, and loneliness, but with limited ability to express or resolve those things either inside the family or outside. The fear of exposure and the family **shame** that would come if they were exposed, keeps the entire family locked in this destructive cycle.

In a healthy family the movement is continually toward health, healthiness, healthy living, love, thankfulness, and obedience, which flows out of the sense of gratitude. Their focus on life is positive. They're not denying reality, because they realize that negative circumstances can happen to anyone. Functional families tend to remain positive even in the midst of difficult situations believing: "Our family is strong enough that together, this can be handled!"

The Five Freedoms – What Is Lost In

Dysfunctional Families

These are the unspoken rules that govern a dysfunctional family. In a dysfunctional family, the motives are compulsive and based in an attempt to meet legitimate needs and avoid pain. Functional families do not seek to avoid pain but are able to embrace its reality, process through it and deal with it. Dysfunctional families cannot process through problems or deal with pain, learning instead ways of avoiding the pain and in extremely bad ways.

The fear of rejection and abandonment is often at the core of this *avoidance/denial* type of behavior. Wounded people (dysfunctional family members) have an overwhelming sense of failure, poor self-esteem and seek their sense of worth through money, power, sex, relationships, the bottle, or drugs. They never actually find the place of peace they desperately seek. This happens because they have been robbed of what has been called the five freedoms, Don't Think, Don't Feel, Don't Talk, Don't Speak of the Truth and Don't Be Intimate[2].

1. Don't Think

In dysfunctional families, a form of thought control is practiced. We observe certain behaviors, or experience hurtful events, but learn at an early age that our thoughts about reality cannot be accurate. Most addicts predetermine what the thought patterns in a home should be and everyone in that home follows those same thoughts, patterns, ideas, and beliefs. Thus they all receive and transmit the same wrong beliefs. So often, children will say (and are taught to do so), "Well, my dad's not drunk, he's sick."

That's what they have heard all their life. "Dad is sick. That's why he can't go to work." It has nothing to do with the fact that he had a fifth of vodka last night and is completely unable to walk. This cannot be seen or discussed, and one's very thoughts are recreated to assert that what is clearly seen cannot be accepted as true.

2. Don't Feel

Many addicts and co-dependent's state, "If I start to feel, I'll feel pain I must avoid the feelings and the expression of feelings." Usually there is

---

[2] Bradshaw, John.

one member of a dysfunctional family system that carries the vast majority of the feelings for the whole family. And usually it is one of the children. That's why, when interviewing families, I will ask each family member to please tell me what the family feeling is. The five primary feelings are: happy, sad, angry, hurt, or scared. Often, I will hear "happy", "happy", "happy" all in turn, until Jr. says, "angry," "fearful," or "hurt."

The latter is usually the true underlying emotional state of family. When presenting this feeling back to the family as a whole, they often drop their heads (in shame) and agree that this is in fact the real feeling of the family. The counseling goal becomes understanding where that feeling came from and why it is there, and why is it not okay to express true feelings within the family. In the process we begin to discover the unwritten rules, myths, and games being experienced in the family.

To talk about the feelings that were previously repressed is an essential aspect of the healing process. Often, the abuser in the family is the only one with permission to express emotion, especially anger, and this person can express it any way they want to, towards whoever they want.

3. Don't Talk

In a dysfunctional family, it is especially dangerous to talk outside the family. Talking creates fear that someone will find out what's really going on which may attack or destroy the family system. Many times the family members will unconsciously keep the truth about the addict from coming out in an attempt to salvage what is left of a broken family system. They do not want to face their situation. There is significant denial which is one of the primary components keeping the addict stuck in their addiction.

Family members may want to keep quiet out of fear that the addict will explode with anger. Dysfunctional family members live in dread that the addict will be either drunk or belligerently out of control, reacting by shutting down emotional expression. If you've ever been in a situation where you know consistently, near the same time every day, that you might face painful abuse, you tend to shut down in order to survive.

People experiencing this emotional blackmail stop thinking, talking, feeling and focus on survival rather than their own emotional **developmental** and familial growth. They wouldn't dare talk about the family problems, are unable to share their feelings or **grieve** over their losses. They just survive day to day somehow. However, they survive without learning necessary skills for healthy living. The alcohol or drug addiction impacts and imprints into the family these very certain patterns on their mind, will, and emotions.

4. Don't Trust

The ability to trust is the foundation of all relationships.

In dysfunctional family systems, members learn that they cannot trust anyone because their primary caregivers are not trustworthy.

When a child hears the promise, "We are going to go fishing this weekend," they know that the chances of that happening are similar to the chances of a snowball in hell! Unfortunately, the co-dependent usually covers for the addict, which makes the problem even worse. Over time, this establishes a diabolical pattern, stripping trust from the child's heart. If they can't trust their parental caregivers, can they really ever trust any authority figure, the police, teachers, or even their own friends? This frequently leads to isolation and intense loneliness. No one who gives their word can ever be trusted it seems. They experience life alone, abandoned, rejected, and lost. In treatment, these are the feelings which will be talked about consistently when they finally begin to share their *family trauma*.

Intimacy Lost

Lack of intimacy brings with it an inability to create adequate bonds or **attachments** to people in general. In order to grieve, there has to have been an adequate attachment to be able to experience a sense of loss from. In many cases, co-dependents have never had adequate attachment. Thus when they experience the loss of a family member or other relationship it becomes just one more loss piled upon another. Grieving becomes hindered, mourning impossible, and the ability to let go of what has happened in their family is stifled. They carry this same *amnesia*, and the same rules, into the next family system. All of this occurs at a family's unconscious level and is assumed to be normal for all families. It is all they have ever known, it must be normal.

Defining Normalcy

A story has been told regarding the concept of normalcy in the context of abnormal social conditions:

A preacher was visiting New York City and wanted to visit Central Park. Having hailed a yellow cab and taken the cross town trip from his hotel to the park, he paid the driver $45 for the trip and exited the cab thinking, "The prices for things in this town are enough to drive one crazy."

Not long after beginning his journey on foot through the park, he encountered a man sitting on a park bench who appeared to be plucking something from the air surrounding him and placing "it" in his shirt pocket. When asked, "What are you doing?" the sitter replied, "I am plucking the stars from the heavens for my collection." A few feet away was another "bench sitter" who was reaching into a brown lunch sack and pulling something very small out and then throwing his hand openly towards the sky. When asked, "What are you doing?" he replied, "Well, it should be obvious shouldn't it? I am replenishing the heavens with new stars to replace this guy's collection of stolen stars. What else?"

About 10 feet further was an athletic individual dressed in running shorts and shoes and holding a nearly empty water bottle. When the pastor asked the runner, "Why are you bouncing your legs up and down? Do you have a leg cramp?" The man replied, "No man. Can't you see, I'm trying to run away from these two guys... they're nuts!"

To act normal in a crazy situation would itself be crazy.

The only way to survive in a crazy situation is to act crazy.

Men who encountered Vietnam with a view that it was not the real world and who merely followed the program presented returned with their psyche fairly intact. When coming home they let go of the crazy world (Vietnam) and returned to the real world (home).

Men who could not adjust in this fashion, trying to be normal (act like home) in that crazy world themselves went crazy, often never again to return to normal. This is one reason why it is so difficult to deal with **post traumatic stress syndrome**, which is what many of society's struggling homeless suffer from. They have never recovered and are still trying to make sense out of something that can make no sense at all.

So it is with most people raised in an addictive family system, along with most active alcoholics and drug abusers who were raised in a dysfunctional family system. Many have played the part of **victims** and **victimizer** in a sense.

Because of their upbringing, these individuals have a limited concept of what normal is. Thus they will suffer from certain aspects of post traumatic stress disorder as they seek to interface with the normal world. Included with this is much denial, internalized pain, with a limited ability to process through or mourn the loss of childhood and relationship.

Intimacy development is predicated on trust, honesty, mutual sharing, respected boundaries and mutual respect, consistently (not perfectly) experienced over time. Since dysfunctional families, especially alcoholic and drug abusing families are unable to provide this consistent care, intimacy development in adulthood (so vital for young adult development) is most difficult to achieve.

The result is often seen in a multitude of relationships or violence within a single relationship in an attempt to cope. Even if the co-dependent child or spouse can see their patterns of intimacy, avoidance and relational sabotage, they are powerless to change the patterns, lacking the skills necessary. Those tools needed for healthy intimacy development have been stripped away. New skills must be learned after a grieving process is accomplished and thinking must be adjusted by the Word of God.

Many have said, "If they just quit drinking, quit doing drugs, everything is going to be fine." However, there's a major difference between living dry and being sober. Though the addict is dry, sobriety through use of proper coping skills is non-existent. That's why in most **Twelve Step Recovery Programs**[3] today they talk about stage one recovery, stage two recovery, and stage three recovery. Stage one is to stop the behavior. Stage two requires letting go of the past, and dealing with the five freedoms that have been stolen from them or they have stolen from others, etc. Stage three equates to helping others with their recovery. Most alcoholics and drug addicts only get through stage one. They get clean or they get dry but they really never learn to change the internal thinking, living out their lives in a less than whole fashion, often with a permanently impaired self-image.

The God-given Appetite

God created us with appetite. He created us with the need to eat, to drink, to rest, to create as our Creator has, and to express our individuality. God created us in his image and likeness. My friend, Don Crossland states that the image of God carries the likeness of God and the dominion of God. The only thing he told mankind not to do was eat of the fruit of the

---

[3] For more, see DeKoven's, *12 Steps to Wholeness*, Vision Publishing.

knowledge of good and evil. Of course, they disobeyed. From there disobedience came vulnerability, a sense of shame, the need to hide and various defense mechanisms. But appetite has always been a part of who we are as human beings. That is, whether Christian or not, as human beings we remain with legitimate, God-given needs that the Lord intends be satisfied.

Jesus did not deny the needs of his humanity. He stated that those who hunger and thirst after righteousness would be filled. Not that his followers would stop eating or drinking natural food. He talked about himself as being the bread of life but broke physical loaves to feed 5,000. He put the appetite in proper priority, as seeking those things that are above are more important than those things that are merely of the earth. The Pharisees called Him a drunk and a glutton because he ate and drank with sinners. Eating and drinking are natural human needs, which are good, ordained of God and legitimate. It is when appetite goes awry that it leads to addiction.

The Wilderness Example

In the book of Exodus, we read the story of the children of Israel as they are delivered from Egypt. God's plan was certainly not for them to wander in the wilderness for forty years, but because of their disobedience, lack of faith, and unwillingness to enter into the promised land when God intended them to do so, they perished in the wilderness over a period of forty years.

In Numbers 11, we see the complaining of the people. Verse one says,

> *"Now when the people complained, it displeased the LORD; for the LORD heard it, and His anger was aroused. So the fire of the LORD burned among them, and consumed some in the outskirts of the camp. Then the people cried out to Moses, and when Moses prayed to the LORD, the fire was quenched. So he called the name of the place Taberah, because the fire of the LORD had burned among them."*

God's chosen people were complaining as people will usually do when things get a bit uncomfortable. They were in the desert, away from their familiar surroundings. They had been accustomed to Egypt, being born as slaves in that land. But Egypt was not exactly a garden spot either. Except for the area right around the Nile delta, many areas in Egypt were quite desert-like. However, Israel had become addicted to the lifestyle they had learned in Egypt. They were not used to the lifestyle of a nomad and had trouble adjusting. In verse four it says,

> *"And the rabble who were among them had greedy desires. And also the sons of Israel wept again and said, who will give us meat to eat? We remember the fish which we used to eat free in Egypt. The cucumbers and the melons and the leeks and the onions and the garlic and now our appetite is gone."*

These men (and probably their wives) bitterly complained because they still had an appetite for the old food and their old life of Egypt. It was as if slavery was great, as long as they could eat pizza!

God had provided for them Manna from heaven; fresh water from the rock, perfect sustenance, even if it was not the world's most exciting diet. God had provided for them perfect food that satisfied the real body hunger that they had. Every vital nutrient they needed was contained in God's perfect food, yet they were still craving things that they had formerly enjoyed. They did not lose the desire for the old things. When we journey with God in the wilderness, we will not lose our appetite for the old things. But, God has adequate and abundant provision in store for us.

The devil no doubt there to tempt them, reminding them of their old life, and the dining delights of slavery.

There was nothing wrong with their hunger. They were not condemned for being hungry or thirsty, but were judged because they were unwilling to accept the provision of God. People that abuse alcohol and drugs have developed a slave's appetite for things highly destructive to God's ultimate purpose for them. Rebellion follows such discontent. In the sixteenth chapter, the third verse, we read:

> *"They gathered together against Moses and Aaron and said to them, 'You take too much upon yourselves, for all the congregation is holy, every one of them, and the LORD is among them. Why then do you exalt yourselves above the assembly of the LORD?'"* (Numbers 16:3)

Rebellion

When appetite moves into the driver's seat of behavior, it often leads to rebellion. The people of Israel's desire was to do their own thing. Going back into slavery was their focus. The spiritual dynamic underlying substance abuse seen from this biblical example is that substance abuse is a form of rebellion. The Bible says in 1 Sam 15:23

> *"For rebellion is as the sin of witchcraft, and stubbornness is as iniquity and idolatry."*

Ultimately, we can see that substance abuse is a form of rebellion. It's a rebellion against the goodness of God and His current provision for our legitimate appetites. I do not know of one drug addict or alcoholic who has not demonstrated an angry stance towards legitimate authority. Legitimate needs unmet always lead to experimentation, which feels good and right, temporarily meeting a legitimate need and anesthetizing the wounds of the soul. But continued usage of the substance over time leads to compulsive addictive behavior.

Starving Norman

When Norman came for counseling, it was under duress. His wife had given him the ultimatum… "Stop smoking dope or you're out!"

Norman related to me a common story of his repeated early childhood disappointments, an absent and often cold father, and an inconsistent mother. Though he was "born again" as a child, the pressure of his peers and pain in his heart had led to early adolescent experimenting with marijuana. He had tried many different things, drank some beer on occasion, but had become truly devoted to one drug of choice.

In assessing his level of addiction, I found he had a family, good job, no major law violations, and friendships (all surrounding drugs, of course) which were many years in length. His only conflict (no guilt due to a seared conscience) was with his wife who complained of his lack of responsibility, along with limited affection and care for her and the children. He seemed to love dope more than anything.

When raised in a family where one is taught by demonstration and open behavior that right is wrong and wrong is right, people tend to get pretty up side down in their view of the world. This explains the phenomenon that often occurs when alcoholics or drug addicts come to Christ. They come to church and love all of the attention, love, and nurturing that they initially receive. But after a season, when they become just a "normal member" of the church they start desiring the old things. Though saved, they require more and deeper relationship because they are internally needy, and highly dependent. The only way they know to survive in times of great need is through engaging the past behaviors that have worked. What they want is someone to care for them, to fix their wounds. Recovery rarely happens overnight. Frequently a repetitive pattern for alcoholic or drug addict who is going through the process of change will be seen.

This was true with Norman as well. He was saved, and his spirit was alive in Christ but his soul still needed tremendous transformation. He had no root or foundation of truth to understand basic right and wrong, nor the power to choose right. His underlying unconscious foundation said that, "Wrong was right. Cheating worked. Stealing worked. Only getting caught was bad." When a person is saved with this mentality it carries over into their Christian experience. Their mind must go through a "wilderness experience[4]" where the old can die of and the new can take root and produce.

Norm, as all compulsive people, needed to be retaught, reparented at a foundational level. He needed years, not weeks of unconditional love and support. To a large extend, this is exactly what happens in well run, Christ centered Twelve Step Programs.

1 John 2:16 states,

> *"For all that is in the world, the lust of the flesh, the lust of the eyes and the pride of life is not from the Father but is from the world."*

It has been said, "Desire inflamed is appetite untamed." When a desire for something goes out of control, human beings tend to "overdo it." This comes from the lust of the flesh.   Desires and appetites must be governed... a skill to be learned over time.

Appetite gone awry also equals alienation. Typically, the consistent result of repeated alcohol or drug abuse is personal and family alienation. The entire family affected can become alienated from other family, friends, God, and even themselves. This creates a need to hide from the shame, and to deny responsibility in order to protect oneself.

> *"But he that sinneth against me wrongeth his own soul: all they that hate me love death,"* *(Proverbs 8:36).*

---

[4] See *40 Days to the Promise: A Way Through the Wilderness* by DeKoven.

A person can't sin against their self much more than injecting a deadly poison into their body. Obviously that is what alcohol, drug abuse, and nicotine addiction are. These substances are poison to the body. It's self-punishment. *"All they that hate me love death."* They are related to a hatred of God (humankind was created in the image of God) and rebellion, combined with self-loathing, and self-rejection.

The Root

Frequently there is a narcissistic injury involved in self-destructive, compulsive behavior. Narcissism is a state of self-absorption. The word narcissistic comes from Greek mythology, where Narcissus looked into a pool of water and upon seeing his own reflection fell in love with it. Well, Narcissism isn't really self-love. It's actually a form of self-hatred. Through an obsessive, neglectful environment they learn that their legitimate needs are not likely to be satisfied. By their actions, they are attempting to make up for what they did not receive. All of their energy is spent on trying to feed the self with things that never satisfy.

> *"But I see a different law and the members of my body waging war against the laws of my mind and making me a prisoner of the law of sin which is in my members," (Romans 7:23).*

In talking with an alcoholic or drug addict, especially if they are in the third stage of addiction (where there is a physical addiction), they will say, "Yes, I want to be free of this." Unfortunately their bodies won't allow them be free. They have become prisoners of the law of sin that leads to death. Sadly, the average life expectancy of an alcoholic is only 55 years. This is due to the increase in sclerosis of the liver, heart problems, cancer and fatal accidents. A recent news report indicated that 50% of all pedestrian deaths are alcohol related. They were drunk or high and was killed while wandering into the path of a moving vehicle. The largest percentage of accidents and deaths in vehicles are alcohol or drug related.

> *"Just as they did not see fit to acknowledge God any longer, God gave them over to a depraved mind to do those things which are not proper,"* (Romans 1:28)

Christians normally apply this chapter to homosexuality or other forms of sexual sin, but it also fits with any type of compulsive behavior. The mind can become so depraved that God will eventually allow the behavior to continue towards destruction. Unchecked, this becomes the ultimate prognosis of long term addiction.

> *"They struck me but I did not become ill. They beat me but I did not know it. When shall I awake, I will seek another drink,"* (Proverbs 23:35).

How unfortunately true this proverb becomes for the alcoholic.

A Horrible Cycle

Alienation leads to addiction, which completes a cycle. People from dysfunctional families become lost in their own mental and emotional stupor. The co-dependent will experience a sense of fear, alienation, and hurt. Somewhere along the line they find an addictive behavior which temporarily and powerfully satisfies the need. The behavior can involve drugs, alcohol, food, gambling, binge and purge cycles or whatever tends to help them avoid the feelings of alienation, abandonment and betrayal. This cycle makes perfect sense to the typical abuser, "I want what is in that bottle because it helps me to avoid facing the pain. It makes me feel better!" The drug brings temporary relief without a sense of guilt... that is until the next day. In some cases, even that guilt is relieved by the fact that the addict can rarely remember what they did, and if they do remember there is the universally accepted excuse, "I was drunk," "I was high," or "I was not responsible." Perhaps they'll even use the Christian favorite, popularized by the TV comedy shows: "The devil made me do it."

The sense of alienation is only amplified when later they receive the inevitable negative feedback from friends and family. Their guilt creates anxiety. Anxiety is automatically linked to the underlying issues they are trying to avoid. So how do they avoid the anxiety? They return to the behavior which has worked so well in the past.

And the beat goes on…

The feelings that accompany the cycle are abandonment and loneliness. This originates in a narcissistic injury, an injury to their "image of self" usually ingrained by trauma experienced at an early age, which resulted in a lack of proper attachment to a mother and/or a father. If you will, there is a "hole in their soul." Their over-indulgence in the substance of choice demonstrates their poor ego development, inadequate sense of self, fear of failure, rejection, success and death.

Yes, even fear of success can add to the cycle's vehemence. The thinking

31

is, "If I succeed this once, those around me may come to expect me to succeed again. They may stop making allowance for my failures and abandon me to 'go it alone,' which I cannot bear! Or, I may be unable to repeat this potential success and therefore lose all sense of self-esteem I currently have."

The pain and uncertainty of impending success can cause the addict to choose failure as a means of maintaining the "*homeostasis* of ongoing, predictable failure." Whole family systems can even become engaged in a subconscious or intentional effort to circumvent an addict's success in order to maintain the homeostasis of the dysfunctional family system. Their thinking is, "Don't rock the boat!"

There is also the prideful attitude of heart which can sabotage success: "If (he or she) the addict succeeds, I will no longer be needed." Or worse, "I'll show (him or her) how much better I am than them... by making sure they fail and then offering to help or extend my 'loving' support." This is a deadly attitude of condescending pride guaranteed to undermine potential success. These are several of the many reasons why addicts and their support groups may be fearful of potential success. It seems the status quo is desirous to all of us at times... few people want to experience days of change even when it is good for us.

The tormenting fears of facing life without their addiction will keep them locked into their compulsion, as does the pain of depression when the behavior once deemed "helpful" is unavailable or no longer works.

Psalm 32:3-5 notes

> *"When I kept silence, my bones waxed old through my roaring all the day long. For day and night thy hand was heavy upon me: my moisture is turned into the drought of summer. Selah. I acknowledged my sin unto thee, and mine iniquity have I not hid. I said, I will confess my transgressions unto the LORD; and thou forgavest the iniquity of my sin. Selah."*

Unhealthy Shame

The hope for compulsive substance abuse rests in God. It begins with the admission of personal responsibility by all parties involved and a willingness to face, trace, erase and replace the old behaviors with God's greater purposes. This process is easier said than done.

Shame is the most insidious part of the compulsive dance. Shame is the underlying belief that one is damaged beyond repair. When a person begins to feel that internal sense of shame, they immediately desire to anesthetize themselves from the potential pain. The underlying belief that one is a monster, a freak or a wretch keeps them from admitting their need for help and submitting to a process of change.

Have you noticed that when people become dry or clean, moving towards sobriety, that remorse and self-condemnation manifests? This may be a con in the beginning. They may be searching for someone to take care of them, fix them, feed them, diaper them, etc. Ultimately a great deal of true guilt and remorse for the things that they have done must be found and owned up to personally.

Unhealthy shame, the belief that we are indefinitely and eternally flawed beyond reparative love must be identified and targeted for destruction. Shame is a powerful mechanism, used by Satan to keep the abuser or co-dependent bound in their compulsive patterns. The hardest part of therapy, after sobriety has been achieved, is uncovering the root of a person's shame (iniquity) and allowing the healing love of Christ to restore them through consistent, Christian care-giving that flows from a heart filled with God's unconditional love.

Remember, chemical dependency is a compulsion, or a forceful urge, the internal itch that cannot be scratched. It is experienced as an overwhelming urge to drink or use drugs, or a compulsion for sexual release or eating to achieve a desired effect. Initially, the addict is searching for a feeling of euphoria, happiness, and social stability, but in the end they just act to cover up the pain. Eventually the addict will no longer experience the once achieved "high." No matter what, they just can't cover the personal pain. That's why they tend to switch to other drugs, and go back and forth between substances, trying different combinations of drugs, which only speeds up the death process.

In the House

Chemical dependency finds its roots in an environment of co-dependent, dysfunctional family life and proceeds from lesser avoidances of pain to greater ones.

The pattern begins in the family system and is usually modeled by members within the family. The modeling is so powerful, as illustrated in this Bible story from I and II Kings:

King Ahab was raised by his father Omri,[5] a King who did great wickedness in Israel. Ahab would no doubt accompany the evil King in his many duties. When Omri worshipped idols Ahab would have been with him, observing dad. He learned early on, "How real men behave." In II Kings it says, *"And Ahab sinned even greater than his father Omri."* In fact, the Bible says Ahab sold himself to sin. He learned these patterns when he was small, leading to where they were great as he became older. He repeated the behaviors that he had observed.

The reactions of men and women raised in substance abusing homes range from total abstinence (usually crusading against all usage of alcohol), to codependency (marrying an addict, unconsciously sensing, "I know how to deal with an alcoholic/drug addict") or becoming one themselves.

Ahab, it appears, took the later route and married a raging idol worshipper (Jezebel) and experienced double the dysfunction as a result. What a mess Ahab made of his family, nation and the people of God in general.

Compulsive behavior is a form of an avoidant response to the stresses of daily living. The learned patterns are built into the dysfunctional family system. Unless one is born into a loving Christian family where everything went practically perfect, we are all likely to pass some measure of dysfunctional behavior on to our children. However, the patterns transferred through compulsive family systems are powerful, deeply engrained

Every Christian is to be constantly growing, being conformed to the image of Christ. Thus we are not to beat ourselves up over difficulties. If it was possible to create perfect parents that would create perfect children there wouldn't be a need for salvation. But obviously, there is always a need for salvation no matter what family system we were raised in.

Chemical dependency invariably flows from a deep wound that needs healing. There is deep psychological pain that requires a dependent relationship, which is more powerful than the original problem. Ultimately, this dependency must be placed on Christ and His Church. Although at times, the church or its members can prove unreliable, Christ can always be depended upon for mankind's deepest needs.

Most people are seeking that more powerful dependency.

Let's illustrate this with Dick and Jane. They came from a typical

---

[5] See, *I Want To Be Like You, Dad* by DeKoven.

American family system. As a typical American, Dick was raised in a dysfunctional family. He did not receive an adequate loving attachment to his mother or father. Careers seemed to mean more to Mom and Dad than kids! He observed dysfunctional patterns and experienced rejection, abandonment and betrayal creating a deep festering wound in his soul. As a man, he has learned to deny his wound and need for love and even though he may not have acted out in terms of drinking or drugs, he remains a wounded man, in need of deep healing. His years of denial have led to an absence of awareness regarding his own deep and legitimate needs.

Jane was raised in an actively alcoholic family. She also has a similar gaping hole in her soul and is looking for that one wonderful, powerful relationship that will heal her deepest though shamefully hidden wound.

What is Dick looking for? A mother that will care for him, nurture him, love him, be totally trustworthy, able to take all of his anger and resentment and say, "Honey I still love you, beat me some more please."

What is Jane looking for? Superman! A man able to consistently love her in spite of foibles, unconditionally care for her, soothe her hurts, dry her tears.

And what do they both find? The Bible says, *"If the blind shall lead the blind will they both not fall into the ditch?"* They have been blinded by the patterns they have learned and the painful wounds in their souls. Inevitably, without intervention, they are destined (if their relationship survives) to pass on the symptoms, shame and compulsivity they inherited to the next generation.

Dick and Jane are looking for someone who will perfectly fill the void in their soul. Is there anything wrong with what they're searching for? No! They are searching for what will satisfy their absolutely desperate need for healing and unconditional love. The problem is that neither of them, in themselves, have enough power to turn on a 30 watt light bulb. Because of their subsequent wounds and shame they cannot provide the love required and are destined to repeat similar patterns, unless there is outside intervention, which must include God.

However, God is not enough. Many people who come from addiction will fall in love with Jesus. Their statement becomes, "It is just Jesus and me," and they become addicted to their own feelings of being high with Jesus. This may be good at the start, and an addiction to Christ is certainly preferable. However, without healthy human relationships in the Body of Christ, the full healing will never come. You cannot separate the head from the body if you want to have life.

The Stages of Addiction

The **first stage to addiction** is experimenting and learning. Nobody becomes an active alcoholic unless they drink. You can still have alcoholic thinking without being an active alcoholic if you never take a drink. The addictive "hole in the soul" is there either way. At some point the addict will begin to experiment and learn the effect of the substance. The new user is generally encouraged to try drugs and alcohol by someone the addict desires acceptance from or as an escape from pain. They will usually start out "light." Very few people actually start with heroin unless they live in the inner city.

Experimenting then leads to the second stage of addiction, development of a "bond." However, the bond is not with people, it is with the substance. Addicts develop an intimacy with their drug of choice. At this stage the abuser begins to obsess about their drug, longing for it. They will talk about the drug as if it were a lover, or their best friend. They can't wait until the next time that they can get buzzed because it was such a wonderful experience. Over time these bonded addicts want to experience more so they increase their intake.

In the **third stage of addiction**, the addict begins seeking for more opportunity to abuse the drug. At this stage the addict begins to seek users of the substance socially. These people are not just experimenting, they have allowed it to become a part of their lifestyle. Usually they will establish limits on their usage for a season. On occasion they might use to the point of excess, but it's not a continuous state. For instance, weekend binges become the norm, with limited use during the week. At this stage, the user may experience some disruption of their work, school, social life and schedule, but there are limited consequences for usage because it is still strongly socially reinforced.

The **fourth stage of addiction** is the obsessing stage, with a pre-occupation with getting high or drunk. They begin to compulsively use the substance with periodic loss of control. They frequently break their own "rules." They might say "I'm only going to use a certain amount," but end up smoking pot all day long. They're still trying to set rules, to control the drug, but they consistently run through their own stop signs. They usually

36

feel a sense of guilt and shame but tend to project their self-loathing onto others. This leads to the breaking of relationship after relationship. At this stage rationalization, justification and denial are in full swing.

The **fifth stage of addiction** is that of being consumed by the drug. They're no longer using the substance, the substance has the user. They're addicted. Now the user must use the drug to feel "normal."

One result of this high level of abuse is despair. The user will often begin to fight suicidal ideation. The addict feels so badly about their life, but are hopelessly gripped by their own behavior. Suicide may appear to be the only viable route of escape to the addict. Their despair and depression will swing to blame and projections of responsibility which lead to more shame and more usage of the substance in a useless effort to kill the pain.

For most addicts, disruption in the major areas of life including work, relationships, legal problems, and health deterioration become evident. They may start losing jobs, or become unable to function in school. Relationships breakdown because they are unable to maintain them. If they are married, their abuse may lead to divorce or domestic violence. Health will eventually break down through accidents and illnesses caused by the excessive use of the substance. Legal problems may ensue such as DWI's or DUI's (**D**riving **W**hile **I**ntoxicated or **D**riving **U**nder the **I**nfluence). During the consuming phase of the addictive cycle, life becomes nothing more than a vicious cycle. It is rarely at this final stage that a counselor will encounter a client before death or permanent disability. Hopefully, intervention will occur at an earlier and more treatable phase.

Not all substance abusers must hit rock bottom before treatment begins. However, knowing the stages is essential as you begin the counseling process.

Chapter One Questions for Discussion

1. What are the five primary emotional needs? Why are these important?
2. List and discuss the five freedoms and their importance in family life.
3. What can the pain and uncertainty of impending success cause the addict to do?
4. What are the five stages of addiction?

Chapter Two

In The Counselor's Office

In the counseling office, there are several barriers that may be encountered with a client. It is possible to break through these barriers to see the real person, but it takes time and effort on the counselor's part. It is not easy to see all of these barriers, but they are ever-present, especially when dealing with substance abusers who have been using from an early age.

The First Barrier - Denial

Denial is not recognizing or admitting a problem in spite of the adverse consequences and evidence to the contrary. Denial is subtle. When one begins to live a lifestyle of deceit, the deceit eventually becomes a part of the thought processes of the person. The mind can become warped, reprobate over time. When the client says, "I don't have a problem with drinking. I can quit at any time I want," they truly believe it. They're thoroughly convinced in their own mind. If you were to say, "let's do an experiment and see," they would probably be able to win the experiment for a season but ultimately they cannot stay away from the substance. Frankly, they don't want to. It's their lifestyle, and they have become self-deceived. Take a look at the James perspective,

> *"Wherefore lay apart all filthiness and superfluity of naughtiness, and receive with meekness the engrafted word, which is able to save your souls,"* (James 1:21)

It's important to note what James is saying and what James is not saying. James is saying that everybody has a certain amount of filthiness and wickedness within them, even when they are spirit filled. We all have issues of the heart that must be dealt with. James is speaking to Christians very directly here: "deal with the issues of your heart!" This can be done when we humbly submit ourselves to the Word of God, acting on it in obedience.

With denial there is an inability to be either meek or humble. Grandiose thinking is one of the primary characteristics seen in substance abusers. Proclaiming their ability to do great exploits, they often over exaggerate

40

their capabilities. They are unable to humbly receive truth. They will admit that they've had a problem only if they're caught by the law or if faced with a painful divorce, but this is only momentary remorse.

People in denial will often make an initial confession of responsibility, but lack sincerity. As a result, they get right back on the treadmill to destruction, since deep down they do not believe they truly have a problem. The problem they have is only that they've been caught. They can temporarily humble themselves, even feign a conversion experience, but only time will tell if they mean it from the heart.

Were they sincere?

Yes, they were sincere as far as sincerity can take them, but they have little depth of soul or character. Addicts can put on any face they need in order to survive in a certain situation, afterwards returning to the same exact place they were before.

"As a dog returns to his vomit...(Proverbs 26:11) so does a drunk to his drink. Now James said, *"...receive the word implanted, the truth, which is able to save your souls,"* (James 1:21).

Relapse is a major problem in treatment and it's prevention is a major component of the counseling process. It is complete wholeness and permanent transformation that God intends. This comes by the Word of God being implanted in the addict's soul (James 1:20). The Word implanted in the original Greek text means, "to be pounded in." That's why you can read the Word to an alcoholic or drug addict without much initial impact. They have such shallow, or in some cases rocky soil, that you've got to pound in the Word, over and over again to get it where it can produce fruit. That's why it takes such a long time to see true re-habilitation in the case of a hard core alcoholic or drug addict.

Rehabilitation efforts must be in direct proportion to the length of abuse and depth of character. One must plow up the soul's fallow ground in an addict and prepare their heart. It takes a long time and hard work to bring them to a place where they're willing to receive the Word and even then it must be pounded down into them so it can take root. When properly rooted in love, God's Word will bring forth good fruit. First you must get past the denial for them to begin to receive. The Word's good fruit will emerge. As long as they're playing the con, they're not going to receive the truth or act on it.

> *"But prove yourselves doers of the word, not merely hearers who delude themselves,"* (James 1:22).

The Man In The Mirror

Alcoholics and drug addicts are hearers who constantly delude themselves. Even when they're saying "Yes, I know. I've got to quit drinking, and I'm going to do that. I know, I'm going to quit. I'm going to quit tomorrow." In their heart they say: "Thank God tomorrow never comes." The addiction and compulsion continuously draws them to return to their substance, to anesthetize their mind and mask their feelings.

> *"For if anyone is a hearer of the word and not a doer, he is like a man observing his natural face in a mirror; for he observes himself, goes away, and immediately forgets what kind of man he was."* (James 1:23 – 24)

One of the requirements for working with addicts, whether in AA groups, or as a clinical therapist, one must be direct, and often harsh to break the cycle of denial. A counselor must call the addict on their "con act" in a most direct manner. The counselor cannot give any latitude to the addict. Black and white is all they can handle. If given shades of gray, as is true with any character disorder, they are going to slip through that crack where a positive therapeutic outcome is unlikely.

The addict must have a clear and absolute directions, such as, "I said be hear at such and such a time." If they're not there, then action must be taken such as turning them into their probation officer. This is the only proven way for many to learn and function.

That's why one recovering alcoholic will "get into another one's face." Listening to them one might think they were extremely angry with each other, but truthful confrontation works. The truth is it is love that dictates the need for the counselor to be challenging and blunt.

Some might say, "Well, that's not very Christian." Nothing could be further from the truth! It is the only thing that works. The counselor must be able to break through the addict's denial so that the client will look into the mirror and remember who they really are.

Many times the addict does not remember what they see when looking into reality's mirror. Addicts come to see themselves as societal victims.

Many are completely convinced of their victimization and their right to behave as they do.

Again, the counselor must be able to break through the denial, at times necessitating **intervention**. Intervention is a therapeutic technique designed to create a forced choice for the abuser. A specialist in intervention will bring the boss, the family, the hospital and significant others in the addict's life together and say, "Here is your choice. You can go into treatment tonight, or you lose your family, your job, and everything else that you ever wanted. It's up to you. What do you want?" Of course if a threat is given, it must be followed-through!

A forced choice is often necessary to thrust someone into treatment. This technique, which is somewhat of a last resort, will often but not always bring the addict face to face with themselves, and with the knowledge that their choice is critical, with much to lose. This form of pressure and crisis can force even recalcitrant people to look in the mirror of reality. But even when they do, they see themselves through tainted eyes. This is because they're whole internal mechanism has been warped by the abuse of substances.

On Defense

Defenses against the ills of the world and attacks against our worth are inherited from our ancestors. Even Adam and Eve in the garden of Eden used primitive defenses, such as denial, rationalization and projection of blame when caught in direct disobedience to God (see Genesis 3).

With the substance abuser, the defenses they often use include the following:

Rationalization is the use of socially accepted but untrue explanations for inappropriate behavior. These include: "I was having a bad day. My boss, my wife, if you were married to that battle axe wouldn't you drink?"

These may seem socially acceptable because most of us can relate to momentary times of despair when we would like to avoid pain. So it is socially reasonable to attempt rationalization in the face of loss of self-esteem. Addicts are filled with a whole bag full of "socially acceptable" explanations which are untrue. In other words, they always have a good reason for why they do what they do. And, of course, it's never them. Nor is it their own personal choices but circumstances or others who have caused their problems.

When an abuser is cornered they will project blame on others for their failures or dysfunction. Projection occurs in any dysfunctional family. Even in a counselor's own life, the initial response when doing something that may be wrong is to try and figure out who else to place the blame upon. The projection of blame is used to avoid the pain of punishment.

If a person feels that they are caged or trapped, they may blame with great anger and emotion. Tears will often accompany this blame. "It's not me, it's them. Look what they've..." It's convincing. Of course, substance abusers are very good at projection. They've convinced many people in the process of learning how to protect and escape responsibility. They blame others for their dysfunction or their failures, often exploding with anger towards anyone who would try and hold them responsible for their behavior.

Repression is an unconscious exclusion from one's conscious mind of unbearable thoughts, experiences or feelings. Repression will eventually lead to a generalized sense of guilt. Most abusers have this generalized sense of guilt, but they constantly repress this feeling. In fact, black outs (the loss of consciousness due to excessive drinking) are a chemically induced form of repression. The abuser cannot remember what they did during a drinking/drugging time. Generally blackouts are the last stage of alcohol addiction, where there is a physical manifestation of the lifelong process of trying to forget everything from the past.

Suppression is to push away unpleasant feelings and events into the background. However, suppressed memories can be recalled. When something is truly repressed, it can't be remembered unless it is brought to remembrance through a process of inner healing or hypnosis. Suppressing a memory is a willful process which becomes a lifestyle for many abusers.

Withdrawal is deliberate avoidance. In it, people deliberately avoid communication with those around them. It is an avoidance of intimacy. This avoidance is rooted in a fear of rejection and abandonment. Many alcoholics and drug addicts emotionally and physically withdraw from others. They try to remove themselves from close relationships partially because they don't want to "get busted," and partially because of their fear of rejection.

They are caught in quite a web! They deeply need relationship, closeness and genuine intimacy but are unable to experience it. Initially, the substance of choice may have been used to create courage for intimacy. However, in the long run it only creates false bonds, transitory in nature, and ultimately emptiness.

44

Regression is a reverting to attitudes, feelings, beliefs, behaviors that belong to an earlier developmental stage. Most abusers, even when not under the influence, tend to act in an immature fashion. This is usually linked to the early adolescent period since that is the age they began to abuse the substance in most cases. Alcohol and drugs quite literally arrest the normal developmental process and produce a form of mental and social retardation.

This explains the phenomenon often seen when someone is converted to Christ, and though clean of substance abuse, will have interactions with people that tend toward the silly and immature. They are reverting to where they "left off" developmentally. This is especially seen where genuine and affectionate feelings are being expressed. Further these same people will frequently act out in order to gain years of lost attention. If someone from the opposite sex were to show interest in them, they become either overtly shy, or act inappropriately forward, similar to that of a 13 year old's behavior. If a counselor is unaware of the fact that their social development may have been arrested when they began to abuse substances, they could become easily upset at their suddenly immature or inappropriate behavior. "Let the addict grow up naturally" would be the watchword here.

The great need for addicts is to experience steady growth through the developmental phases God ordained. It is here that they must learn how to give to others and live responsibly, taking care of their own needs and being responsible to others. They must learn to be faithful over little, and eventually they can learn faithfulness over much. Simple tasks such as getting up and taking care of daily business must be learned. Many substance abusers need a complete lifestyle change. Though they live in a 35 year old body with 35 year old intelligence (in most cases), they have the emotional and psychological make-up of a 13 year old child. This makes the counseling process tedious at best and like a minefield at worst. Thus, it is important to remember that he who is forgiven much loves much… They are worth the effort if they are willing to pursue change. It is certain that God believes the addict is worth the effort. That is why He sent Christ and us as well; people are worth the effort.

A final defense mechanism to be considered is Conversion. This is an expression of emotional conflict through physical symptoms. A conversion reaction helps to avoid, through physical symptoms (generally pain), what is actually occurring emotionally. The pain that the addict experiences is real. Many alcoholics and drug addicts who have been clean for a long time will sometimes suffer from forms of conversion reactions or psycho-somatic illness.

Anyone who has counseled an alcoholic who was a hard core addict, will hear stories of what they call "slips." A slip is where they will like wake up in the morning with the taste of alcohol on their tongue. They have a memory that they were out bingeing the night before. This causes them great panic because they had been dry and sober and they fear that they must have fallen off the wagon. Later, they learn that it was just a brainslip. This is a part of the transformational process of the chemicals in the brain. A brainslip is a release of memories so vivid that they actually felt as though they had been drunk.

This type of reaction to long term drug abuse is one part of "reaping what has been sown." No matter how wonderful salvation experience someone may have, there is still a price most will pay for years of abuse to mind, body and spirit. But before helping the addict to face their future, you first must help them resolve the past, which starts through removing of the various masks they have come to fashion and wear.

Chapter Two Questions for Discussion

1. What is the first barrier a counselor must help the addict to confront and conquer?

2. Can anyone in denial be meek or humble?

3. Can an addict be sincere?

4. Rehabilitation efforts must be in direct proportion to what?

5. Why is it sometimes necessary for a counselor to be direct, often harsh, in dealing with the addictive process?

6. Discuss intervention and its place in treatment.

7. What are the six most often used defenses by an addict? Briefly explain each.

Chapter Three

The Masks We Wear

When I talk about masks I am talking about the basic defense mechanisms which are manifested in the average person.

Basic defenses used to cope, employed excessively over time, lead to permanent masks. A mask is worn in an attempt to hide guilt and shame, but is not strong enough to keep the abuser from self-hatred and resultant self-punishment, which leads to the cycle of addiction. In order for healing to occur, the counselor must be able to get behind the mask. Unfortunately, alcoholics and drug addicts don't have just one mask. They have many different masks and they have learned how to switch them in times of need. It's almost automatic for them. They use their masks to cover themselves and to keep from being exposed to the pain in their soul.

In fact, one of the prominent masks used is that of confession. This is where the abuser tells you anything, with great emotion, yet still tells you nothing. To understand the importance of the concept of masks in substance abuse, several are presented here.

Closed communication is a mask. This is an unwillingness to disclose one's self to others. Abusers are rarely open to criticism, be it constructive or otherwise.

A self-effacing attitude can be another mask. Here people are not feeling what they express. Their expression is most frequently what they think they're supposed to say so that others will stop probing further.

With many substance abusers, you can observe repentance at the altar, with weeping, wailing and gnashing of teeth, but it means little. It's just part of the game. It's a mask of manipulation.

Addicts will compulsively attempt to manipulate their environment to keep themselves feeling safe.

Another mask seen often in addiction counseling is the "I can't" mask. This is the great universal excuse. "I just can't, I can't quit, I can't change, I can't do this, I can't. I can't. Why are you making me?" The excuse sounds like it is coming from a child of about 8 years of age. When listening into their conversation, it sounds a bit like this: "Mommy, will you clean up my room for me? Please mommy please? Please? Mommy!" If you listen to the emotional content while speaking with this mask, it says: "I feel helpless, do it for me."

And if you actually do, the addict will internally state, "What in the world is the matter with you, idiot? Why did you do that for me?"

They will have no respect for you, because to them you're just another jerk who they manipulated at will. If you don't do what they want, then they project blame for their hurt and the: "You don't care for me" attitude. This is all part of their unconscious "I can't" and avoidance game.

There is an individual that my mentor and friend Dr. Bohac counseled who worked part time his whole life and was a substance abuser. He was also involved in sexual addiction. The man was "born again," was called to the ministry, but he has never been able to finish what he started. He just can't seem to get it together. His reasons for not finishing anything are all victim oriented (no one helps me). It's just his game.

Substance abusers want what they want and they want it. A substance abuser will call the counselor's office with a request or need and if they can't reach the counselor immediately, they'll go drink or act out because "the counselor wasn't available for them." The counselor must avoid accepting the blame and set boundaries on the client to keep from becoming hooked into their self-destructive game.

Another mask of importance is what we call "What About Me." This mask develops because the abuser as unaware of the needs of others being totally self-absorbed. They're experts at being able to turn any conversation towards their wants or needs. They often turn things around in such a way that even a mature counselor will feel like they really have victimized the poor client. They are completely unaware of the counselor's needs, especially if you're in the counseling role, both in terms of time and other priorities.

It is typical for an alcoholic or drug addict, (even after becoming clean), to be consistently late for counseling sessions. Yet, these same people expect much more than their allotted counseling time in addition to the time you provide. They may become upset when you don't let them borrow your bedroom because their girlfriend is coming over that night. This narcissistic focus on their own life gives them permission to ask for anything.

Thus, the counselor must be cautious. Because the more you give, the more they want. If you say, "Wait a minute, I can't give that anymore," they act as though you were personally attacking them. This again exhibits their lack of contact with reality, a component of the disease and the scorched consciousness of what is fair or reasonable.

In the counseling process it is important to set a start and closing time for each meeting. If you're starting a 7:00 PM group meeting, attendees must know the doors will be closed and locked at 7:10. Though they stand outside and beat on the door, they must learn boundaries and limits. That's the only way they will learn. They learn by having clear rules and boundaries which are enforced separately and consistently over time. They'll do everything they can to break the rules and manipulate you to give them some special deal, but to give in will feed into their underlying pathology.

Thus, the counselor must be careful. We have to be a living example by being able to set and keep our own boundaries. The counselor should only see the client during the time that has been established. For example, I personally give clients who are extremely dependent or co-dependent times when they have my permission to "have a crisis," within the boundaries.

I'll say, "Now, I'll be available for your phone calls and crises during this time and this time. I'm just doing paper work, I'll be happy to talk to you. However, if you call me during the weekend, I'm not going to be there and I won't respond to you." Once they learn that you actually mean it, they will follow your "crisis" rules.

The response abusers often received as children was: "Shut up! Leave me alone." It is quite normal for the counselor to have similar feelings wanting to say, "Shut up! Leave me alone." That's not what they need. They need the counselor to say, "I will see you in five minutes." Of course, we must make sure that we actually see them in five minutes.

Another message that addicts received as children was: "Later!" or, "I'll get to you when I can." The counselor must establish clear boundaries, clear commitments, and then keep them. This establishes a foundation of parental stability that the client can use to begin the process of learning trust. But they will constantly test it. They test and test and test until they can finally feel truly safe. That's why group treatment tends to be better when working with alcoholic and drug abuse clients.

Then there is the "What's Mine Is Mine, What's Yours Is Mine," Mask. The abuser is possessive, yet dependent. They don't really "need," they just "want" and it's okay for them to lie, cheat, and steal to get what they want. They see themselves as survivors. They've learned to survive in highly dysfunctional ways. In this way they literally see what's theirs as theirs and what's yours as theirs as well. If you were to leave five dollars on the counter, and turn your back, then it's no longer yours, it's theirs.

To them, possession is nine tenths of the law, except in their case. They lack a sense of guilt about taking the remaining tenth for themselves. This is because they've learned to be users in every aspect of life.

They're often paranoid over little things. So if you confront them with wrong behavior, the first thing they'll say is, "I didn't do it."

This presents another picture of the client's early developmental stages. It is as though you found a pile of crumbs leading up to the counter, the cupboard door is open, the lid of the cookie jar is off, and the child's hand is in the cookie jar. When you catch the child with the hand in the cookie jar they exclaim, "I was getting a cookie for you Mommy!"

When confronting them about a problem they may actually feel good that they were busted. They may act fearful because they expect rejection and abandonment. However, when you don't reject or abandon them it creates the possibility for healing in terms of trusting relationships. They demand trust, but do not reveal themselves and do not give trust. In fact, these addicts are highly suspicious, becoming enraged if you are suspicious of them and their motives. This is yet another mask.

Ultimately, abusers can become explosive if blamed for something or if held accountable for an area of covenant relationship. They will use all of their masks, switching rapidly from one to another. If we hold their feet to the fire, in a loving way, they will begin to develop a bond with the counselor like they've never had before, which initially frightens them. They've never experienced true relationship.

Finally, they tend to be passive-aggressive, and passive-dependent. This means they don't keep they're commitments and can manipulate others. It's so easy for them to say, "Yes, I'll be there," and then never show up. How do they feel about this? They usually have no feeling whatsoever about keeping their commitments. If we are stupid enough to wait for them, then we deserve what we get. Thus, it is helpful if they have something to lose whenever they break a commitment. This something could be a relationship, a job, some form of legal action, or whatever. If you've got that kind of hook, it's a whole lot easier to work with them than if you don't.

The attitude of an abuser is: "Do unto others, but don't do unto me!" They can talk a good talk, but they don't walk a good walk. They want to be treated in a kind way. Yet they treat others in a despicable fashion with a sense that the world owes them something. Truly, we owe them nothing except to minister tough love through our counseling techniques.

According to ego-psychology, abusers lack a solid ego attachment. This means they have not developed a well-rounded sense of who they are. They may have been victimized, but they do more to victimize themselves and others than what has ever been done to them. That's one way they ward off the feelings of being a victim. They desperately see the wrong when they are victimized but not when they do the same to others.

The last common mask is: "Life is too tough for me," where the focus of life is the fix. They see life as too difficult, and too hard. That's why they go back to their drugs or alcohol, time after time.

Understanding what types of "masks" your client uses to protect him or herself from facing truth is a first step in treatment intervention. Facing the truth head-on is absolutely essential, no matter how painful. Yet, there is so much more the Lord wants to do than merely affix responsibility leading to cessation of the abusive behavior. Thus, we must take the next step, that is, to look behind the mask, and see the root. At the same time, it is our obligation to help trace the origins of the client's deeply felt narcissistic wounds.

Where Did The Mask Come From?

The masks we have described are all basic characteristics one may find in an alcoholic or drug addict's pattern of behavior. The root cause of that behavior is the same for both of them. They have experienced brokenness. Everyone begins at that same place.

It starts with a traumatic event or situation creating anxiety, guilt or shame, which requires the use of defenses for survival. We've covered some of the defenses or masks frequently used. When defenses no longer work, symptoms develop. A substance abuser ultimately creates his or her own symptoms by consuming more and more of their substance. They experience progressive, related complications, which lead to what is referred to as: "limitation in their range of experience."

Traumatic Event or Experience

|

Anxiety

|

Defenses

|

Symptoms

|

Range of Experience Limitation (dysfunctional patterns limiting God's purposes)[6]

Basically, it is the same process regardless of what symptoms may eventually emerge. The goal of counseling is to assist the client to process through and resolve their past defenses, anxiety, guilt, fear and shame. Ultimately, each must be helped to see what traumatic events or dysfunctional lifestyle in which they were raised and have caused them to experience debilitating bitterness, resentment, etc. The counselor helps to resolve the conflicts left from those early developmental years and teaches new, more effective and adaptive behavioral patterns for coping.

The alcoholic or drug addict possesses so many different masks and has often experienced much damage (much of which has been self-induced). It takes much longer to open their eyes to reality than with any other form of behavioral or psychological disorder. It takes longer because they must first become dry and clean. To further complicate the counseling protocol, you may have to work with them while they are still self-medicating. The medication they have been using hurts them and they don't want additional pain. Unfortunately, without a certain amount of pain, worthwhile change cannot be made. Most people embark on the change process because they hurt; not because their life is wonderful. If

---

[6] Developed by Bruce Narramore, Ph.D.

everything was going well in life, there would be no reason to change. There has to be a certain amount of anxiety in order to keep the "heat" on the client regarding the need for further change. This is not always easy to do when you are working with an ongoing, active substance abuser.

If the counselor can assist the addict to find and fully face the truth, looking behind their masks, there is great hope for completing the first step in the healing process. Healing always begins with a good and accurate assessment of the problem.

Chapter Three Questions for Discussion

1. What is a mask? Do alcoholics and drug addicts have only one mask?

2. Name and explain two different kinds of masks.

3. Why must a counselor set and keep boundaries?

4. Which form of treatment works best for alcoholics and drug abusers? Why?

5. What is the first step in treatment intervention?

6. Describe what range of experience limitation is.

Chapter Four

Assessment

Turning in treatment reports is the hardest part of counseling. Even if you're in a private practice, you always want to keep good medical and psychological records of the counseling process. Your diagnosis and everything else discussed in the counseling process should be kept in some kind of permanent record. These records should be securely stored in a safe place where they can be kept absolutely confidential. The information is personal, owned by the client, and not to be given to any other person unless it is subpoenaed by a court of law, or by request of the client for their benefit. Keeping good records will help the counseling process.

Many therapists keep record on tape. They dictate notes for a secretary to type up. This, of course, is alright except that it can damage some aspects of confidentiality. The counselor must safeguard the tape, and ensure that the person typing the notes is trustworthy and fully confidential as well.

Addendum One contains a typical assessment format that can be used as an example. It will provide the student an idea of what assessments should look like when completed on an active client.

The First Stage

Good assessment is the first stage of proper treatment.

The first thing needed, in order to assess a patient properly is to have a complete medical and social history of the patient. With a substance abuser, a full picture of the extent of their abuse is essential. This is not always easy to obtain since the addict is frequently so filled with dishonestly, they will rarely tell the truth. It could hurt!

The counselor must ask very specific questions in order to determine whether or not and to what extent they have abused various drugs or alcohol. In some cases, addicts have been "strung out" for so long they cannot remember the truth. Yet the counselor must make a good faith effort to piece together a clear picture of the patterns of abuse prior to launching into various potential therapeutic interventions.

Along with a history of their substance use and abuse, it is important to know what medical problems have occurred because of the substance abuse and who (if any) their primary care physician is. Obtain a signed release of information form from the client to talk with their physician. Most of the time you will learn that the doctors they refer you to have never even heard of them, or haven't seen them for a long time. These doctors frequently have no knowledge of the substance abuse but can become allies in treatment. If possible, it is good to practice to obtain a full and complete medical history on the client. If possible, a good medical exam for the client is also to be recommended because there is often significant damage the client has done to themselves because of their abuse.

Such information is always vital to ensure proper diagnosis. To treat a medical or psychological problem with spiritual discipline alone can itself be unethical. Sometimes clients may need medication to help in the treatment or during the recovery process. Often they can be significantly depressed and anti-depressant medications can be useful. Further, just as with long term alcoholics, addicts may experience physical withdrawal symptoms (called DT's for short) for short a period. Various tranquilizers can help in reducing these symptoms and painful symptoms that alcoholics and drug addicts experience as part of their "drying out."

The vast majority of people who quit drugs and drinking do so on their own, not using a 12-step or other treatment program. Most will quit because they decide to. Some crisis may precipitate their decision. Nonetheless, it is a personal decision. Usually they will utilize various aids to help them quit. In other words, they will self-medicate, and then get off the medication, finally overcoming whatever it was that they were struggling with.

In an assessment, we will want to know what stressors in the present and from the past have triggered the drinking or drug abuse cycle. There are frequently predictable psychological, family and work-related stressors that motivate addicts in the direction of abusing a substance. It's important to discover exactly what those things are.

Further, it should be discovered what the dynamics are of their present family; or if they are even in a family. What exactly are the dynamics of their family of origin? What are the generational influences, such as learned alcohol abuse from other members of the family system?

The therapist will want to become aware of relationships with family members or friends that the client says were close to them and then lost as a result of the abuse. Often therapists will discover that they were not as close to the addict as they believed they were. In some cases, the addict may have a person, usually not a member of the immediate family that they were very close to. This loss is significant, and will require grieving once sobriety has been accomplished. This very significant loss may have triggered a process called the abuse cycle. Though the information may not be used in counseling at the beginning, remember the gathering of data is essential.

Finally, it is important to probe their spiritual life. What is their relationship with God and with others in the body of Christ? If they are not born again, obviously that's something that we want to lead them toward. Remember that God wants to heal them totally, not just spiritually. The goals are to reestablish a lifestyle conducive to growth, restored relationships and productive life.

One popular assessment tool that is highly effective is called the Jellenic Stages of Alcoholism scale. This tool helps to determine what level of drug abuse your client is involved in. The youth questionnaire (40 questions) is a particularly helpful tool, assuming the addict is honest. It has been found that many adolescents are more honest than adults are. Using this test we can derive a fairly clear picture of the client's level of abuse. It will further describe the history of anti-social behavior, which is often a part of the abuse pattern. That is, the acting out behavior is frequently related to substance abuse.

The Twelve Step Process

One of the most effective; though controversial treatment tools for substance abuse eradication has been the Twelve Step Program and its various permutations. There is no panacea with 12-step groups, just as there is no panacea in any form of counseling. Obviously, the individual must desire to change. If they do not want help, the counselor probably will be unable to effectively help them. We must trust God in the counseling process. Don't be discouraged if you counsel a substance abuser and it does not work out well. Many have processed through numerous counselors and helpers. It may take many more before help is actually received. Don't worry about it. Trust the scriptures that tell us some sow, some water, but God gives the resultant increase.

In working with substance abusers it does help to use a combined approach of individual and family counseling along with 12-step or some other support group program. 12-step programs have been a great benefit to millions. It has helped them to become clean and sober. If you're not familiar with the steps the first few are the most important, but especially step one.

It says, "I have come to a place where I recognize that I am powerless over the substance; whatever it is," (Paraphrased).

Step two states, "I believe there must be a God somewhere." The twelve step program was initially founded by a born again Christian and a God fearing man. The program was effective but professionals wanted to create a program that would not exclude people who did not share a Christian background. Their motivation was very positive. They wanted to work with "whosoever will," without the trappings of religion. Their focus of God was strongly Judao-Christian in viewpoint in the beginning, though it's not always true now today.

The 12-step program of today states we need God as we know Him to be. God is referred to as a "Higher Power." Your higher power could be the door knob! This can lead people into dangerous New Age beliefs, though many have also received Christ through an effective Twelve Step program.

The program acknowledges that the client must come to a place of decision, realize there must be a "higher power" or God who can restore them to sanity. Abusers at the end of their rope can easily take this step.

The third step is, "I turn my life over to God as I know Him." This decision has potential dangers. Turning one's life over to God is good, but leaving the definition of who God is to their individual imaginations can be dangerous.

The process of a 12-step group, and the encouragement received from the group is very helpful. It is a necessity for someone who is struggling to overcome their alcohol or drug addiction. When turning their life around towards God as the "steps" call for, it may not be the God of the Bible. Thus we need to help our clients connect to the God of the Bible.

As Christian counselors our concern is for the client's ultimate healing and salvation. We must remember that the thinking of an alcoholic or drug addict has been damaged severely by abuse. Thus, their ability to fully understand who God really is and how to receive His many blessings can be highly impaired. Though they may have a knowledge of religious terminology, religion can also be one of the many masks they wear to avoid personal responsibility for their recovery.

Step four, in the 12-step program encourages the client to deal with things that they have long since buried. Step four states, "I've done a moral inventory of my life." Theoretically, the abuser will look into the mirror of their life with someone else to help them face who they are and what they have done. This will include both acts and attitudes of anger, bitterness and unforgiveness towards others. Each aspect of this personal, moral inventory is to be written and discussed in detail with a sponsor or counselor. If done honestly, this can be highly therapeutic.

Steps five, six and seven are designed to make amends towards others for moral lapses to deal with the addict's many character defects. First, they turn their past over to God, then seek forgiveness from others, and finally ask for forgiveness while forgiving others. As can be easily seen, this is a process where they systematically work through the underlying root of their addiction, putting off alcohol, while renewing the mind with the eventual goal of helping others to become clean and sober as well. Though 12 step programs can become "New Age-like" it does not mean we should fear them. They are often useful as pre-evangelism tools, and the step or process is easily integrateable into Biblical principles.

As a counselor, we have the option of using many fine Christian 12-step programs that clearly focus on the belief that Jesus Christ can restore all types of people to sanity. In these groups, people turn their lives over to Christ as Savior and Lord. They do an inventory as the Holy Spirit reveals. They deal with the things revealed from a Christian orientation.

Chapter Four Questions for Discussion

1. What is the hardest part of counseling?

2. Why is keeping good records so important?

3. What can be a good method of keeping notes?

4. Why do you need a complete medical and social history of a patient first?

5. How can the use of prescription drugs be helpful to an addict?

6. Why are stressors a factor in substance abuse?

7. What is the main focus of a Twelve Step Program?

Chapter Five

Addiction... Are We All Addicted?

Substance abuse in Western nations is epidemic. It is easy to believe that only certain types of people suffer from addiction. Modern society has many substances to which we've all become at least mildly addicted, but not to the point where we should think of ourselves as drug addicts. It is true, we are not addicts in the fullest respect.

Many of us, however, do take over the counter medications; and many of these drugs and home remedies have been shown to be extremely addictive. Very few people would deny or argue that heroin and cocaine are highly addictive drugs. In past history, however, it was very common for people to take Morphine or heroin on a regular basis for pain. They called it Lognum when it was an over the counter drug. You could walk into any druggist or pharmacist and say I need some Lognum, and they would sell you a whole bottle of it.

Another example would be Immodium. Immodium is an over counter drug. It's a relatively harmless drug, but years ago Americans used Paregoric in its place. This medication was frequently given to babies to shut them up. This was later found to be a big mistake because paregoric had a synthetic morphine in it. I'm sure that some of the "druggies" that are around today may have gotten their start as babies when they were given a little paregoric to ease mom's or dad's anxiety.

Paregoric was wonderful stuff when you had really bad stomach cramps or the flu. This drug was so effective that the next time they got a pain, they would head directly for the medicine cupboard and get the paregoric.

A friend related that their mother-in-law suffered for many years with a stomach problem. She was a die-hard Pentecostal who would not take even aspirin. She had so many stomach problems, living in nearly continual pain. His wife and he were instrumental in getting her started in her addiction. One day they suggested to her, "Why do you suffer like this? Take a little Paregoric. We give it to the babies. It won't hurt you." So she agreed. Her exact expression was, "It's a miracle!"

A Personal Glance At Physical Addiction

My friend and colleague, Dr. Bohac related this story,

> "I can honestly say that one time I was well on my way to being addicted to codeine, which is another lovely drug. After one surgery, for some reason I developed a severe lower back pain. It was terrible. I was in a great deal of pain. My doctor prescribed Tylenol 3, which has codeine in it. When I began taking these, I discovered that where one tablet of Tylenol 3 was very affective in the beginning, I was soon needing to take 2 for the same affect.
>
> After a short while I was taking two of these pills several times a day. One afternoon I totally fell apart. I totally disintegrated and didn't know what was happening to me. A nervous break-down is what I had experienced. I had enough sense to call my doctor who told me to get into the hospital right away. When I arrived they put me to bed and wouldn't even give me aspirin. I realized at that point that what was really happening to me was the result of my body craving this drug that had been prescribed for me by a doctor."

I don't think any of us have a problem today calling codeine a drug, and a dangerous drug at that. It's a substance that can be used or abused. There are times when it won't hurt to have Percadan, and it will help. There are times when morphine will bring a release from excruciating pain. But, we must be aware of the addictive quality of helpful, legal but often overly prescribed medication.

Without Pain

Dr. Brandt is a physician who worked with lepers for many years in South Africa. At present he has a center in Southern Louisiana where he still works with lepers. Many people do not know that leprosy in itself is not the problem that causes the body parts to fall off. We think of leprosy as a disease that eats your fingers away. It's not like that at all.

Leprosy attacks the nerves and the nerve endings. So the person with leprosy develops a lack of feeling in their hands, feet, etc. Where you or I might touch a hot object on the stove, and immediately react with, "Wow, that's hot, be careful," a leper would not feel the heat. They would see a burn afterwards on their hands and then say, "Oh, I guess it was hot. Look what it's done to my hand." If they're in a situation where they were barefoot in some remote area of Africa, they could step on objects that could pierce their foot entirely and they wouldn't know. This would eventually cause infections often leading to amputations.

Avoiding The Warnings

God gave us the sensation of pain to protect us. Pain is the signal that something is wrong. Whether pain is physical or an emotional, is secondary. Pain is God's way of alerting us that something is in need of attention. Through experience and continual bombardment of the popular media, we have all been persuaded to believe that any discomfort experienced should be immediately alleviated with medication. Rather than searching for the root of the pain, we cover it. It has become the American way. It is a dangerous behavior.

A dear friend of mine, his wife, my wife and I went to Disneyland one weekend. We just wanted to get away. Well, my friend used to get this awful heartburn. So he would take some Baking Soda whenever he experienced this. He had been a mail carrier until he retired from the post office. Postal delivery workers as a rule are usually quite healthy people because they must walk a lot. He was a big man, but he looked like he was perfect health.

One day I asked him, "John, have you ever gone in for an examination. Have you ever had a treadmill. Have you ever had an Electro-cardiogram."

He replied, "Oh-no. I don't need that. Just heartburn is all it is."

Well, a few months after later they moved to Oklahoma where they were attending Bible College. One day I received a call from his wife. She said, "John walked into the kitchen this morning experienced some tremendous gas pain. He asked me where the baking soda was and fell on the floor. Dead!

Boom! Like that John was dead. He was having cardiac pain all of this time and had been covering it up with baking soda rather than dealing with it. What we can learn from this is if you take morphine when you actually have a cardiac problem, the pain will disappear. However, the cardiac problem is not gone. You've just cut off the pain that was warning you that something was really wrong. This is extremely important to realize. It is a life or death matter.

If someone is in emotional pain, experiencing great anxiety, they need to do something. If they are experiencing depression, they can go to the doctor to be prescribed anti-depressant medication. Even though the anti-depressants will lift their spirits some, they will still have to deal with the root that's causing the pain. We can't risk leaving our pain in an infected state. Drugs, for the most part, are only a mask to cover pain. We have to recognize that pain is present for a reason: find its root and resolve the problem.

Mind Altering?

Any substance that is mind altering in any way is a drug. For example, Morphine actually alters the mind to the point where it does not feel pain. Tylenol and Aspirin do the same. So do all the other remedies that most of us ingest on a regular basis. These may not be addictive but they are drugs nevertheless. They are mind altering. The purpose of the aspirin or Tylenol is to dull the pain that we're experiencing (thankfully!).

Actually, they don't dull the brain itself, because there is no feeling in the brain. These drugs actually dull the central nervous system, those tiny nerves that go through the body that funnel through the spinal cord and into the brain. The theory is that these mind altering drugs block off a part of the nerve impulse.

With harder drugs, such as heroin, a person must take more and more because when one nerve is blocked off, another one will start to manifest the pain. This is God's way of making sure that you respond to pain and fix the problem if possible. In similar fashion, when arteries that become plugged, will eventually create veins that branch off of the main arteries to make up for the loss of blood flow.

Many people can't get through the morning until they've had at least one or two cups of coffee. We need the caffeine rush! In fact, one of the most difficult drugs to shake is chocolate. In our culture today, prescription medications, caffeine, pain relievers, etc. are all acceptable drugs, even in the Christian community.

Nicotine

Nicotine is one of the hardest (some say THE hardest) addictions to break. Have you ever known people that smoked and wanted to serve God, but no matter how hard they may have tried, they cannot get over the nicotine addiction. Smoking cigarettes really is a very powerful addiction today. Fortunately, I never started smoking. I did, however, live with a mom and dad who smoked religiously until giving their hearts to the Lord. Even then, it was a tough battle that took many months before they were able to kick the habit completely. There are people who love God and are as sincere as they possibly be, but are completely hooked on nicotine. It might interest you to know that one of the founders of AA died from a disease related to smoking. While they could overcome alcoholism, they could not quit smoking!

It is sad how much power this drug has on people. One of the reasons nicotine has such power is the fact that people usually start smoking at an early age. Statistically speaking, there are more youth smokers today than there are youth alcoholics. This is because parents work hard to keep their kids away from alcohol but they don't see as much harm related to cigarettes. It should be noted that one of the primary "money" crops puritans raised was tobacco.

Another "acceptable" addiction in Christian circles is food. There are people who are totally addicted to various foods. For example, they love chocolate. Chocoholics eat chocolate on a binge basis, especially when they are stressed or bored. They crave more, and more chocolate.

Let's never forget that we are in some measure, all addicted, in some way, to various things. Some are addicted to work. Many people have become addicted to sex. We can become addicted to a host of things which are not, in themselves, evil, hurtful or wrong. The problem arises when any behavior becomes the only means for alleviating a pain that needs to be dealt with on another level. This is when it becomes, or leads to, a true addiction.

Nailed To Our Addiction

When we talk about addiction, it's interesting to discover that the Greek and Latin derivations of this word carry the same meaning as being nailed to a cross. In essence, if you are addicted you're nailed, and you can't get off the cross. There is no way in the physical realm that Jesus could have ever come down from the cross on which he was crucified, because His hands and feet were physically nailed to it.

Addiction is more than a small "nailing" habit; it is a dependency on a particular substance to sustain equilibrium in life.

There are many levels of dependence. Helping people who are addicted to become free is an essential part of counseling though it is, at times, a most difficult process. People can be set free by prayer, but until we deal with what originally led them to the addiction that addiction can return.

I have seen this cycle many times. It is discouraging to see people come for counseling or church as alcoholics, nicotine abusers, sex addicts, only to see them continue or return to the addiction. They come to the altar, give their heart to Christ, and God sobers them miraculously. But the sad, horrible, and heart wrenching thing is to see that same person, a few months later right back in their addiction. Prayer is powerful, but sometimes there is more required than prayer alone.

Emotional Arrest

When a person begins to consume alcohol their normal emotional development is arrested. Their body keeps growing but emotionally they become fixated or stuck. They've stopped growing emotionally. This is one of the many problems in dealing with people in groups for addiction. You face adolescent or pre-adolescent behavior living in forty year old bodies.

If you will, they are 45-50 years old, but are hooked on the oral stage of life. They receive their greatest gratification in life from their oral senses: their mouth and their tongue. Why is it that some people eat and eat and eat and eat and eat and eat? It is because they receive so much oral gratification from putting things into their mouth.

There are many who believe that smoking is a problem with oral stage development. There is a need for the smoker to put something in their mouth. You can see this in people who don't smoke cigars but keep one in their mouth all of the time! They do so for oral satisfaction. Next time you see a major league baseball player with a huge wad of tobacco in his mouth, you can say to yourself, "oral arrest."

A family friend was a chain smoker, but when he and his wife decided to have a child, he was smart enough to quit for the child's sake. He first quit smoking cigarettes and went to a pipe, not knowing it was essentially the same thing. The smoke, if inhaled, will kill you just as fast. Finally, somebody convinced him that for his kids' sake he had better not smoke anything. So now he chews up to two boxes of round toothpicks every day. You will never see him today without a toothpick in his mouth, but at least he is not killing himself with tobacco.

Obviously, our friend has a need which is not being met. I say this because it is possible to become stuck in a developmental stage. If you don't deal with it, by growing up or maturing, it will never be resolved. If, as a counselor, you confronted a client stating "You're stuck in the oral, thumb sucking stage of life," he would get furious! The point made is that unless he does something he'll be forever chewing toothpicks from now until the Lord comes. He doesn't even know why he chews toothpicks.

When we consider drug abuse, or for that matter any problem in counseling, the main question should always be: how did they get this way? Remember, all behavior is learned, and can be unlearned. Our goal is to uncover the root, the basic unmet need which is being anesthetized by the addictive behavior. With this information, our next step is to help the client meet their legitimate need in a legitimate, healthy and God honoring way.

Chapter Five Questions for Discussion

1. What highly addictive drugs, under different names, used to be over-the-counter drugs?

2. Why did God give us a sense of pain?

3. What is wrong with just covering pain?

4. Name a few addictive drugs that are acceptable even in the Christian community.

5. Are we all addicted on one level or another?

6. Can a person be set free from their addiction by prayer along?

Chapter Six

Learned Behavior

Human development is a course of study which explores two views of learning in humans: nature and nurture. What part of us is nature (temperament)? Or what part did we inherit from those 23 separate genes from each parent? There is undoubtedly much inherited from our family. This includes our eye color and physical stature; which are proven examples of inherited traits. But is it possible for us to also inherit in some measure aspects of our temperament? The question is, what part of our behavior is based on the nature of our inheritance, and what is based on nurture in the home? How much of our current state of being did we learn from others?

All behavior is learned. Though we may have inherited our temperament with it's too many tendencies or predilections, we must still learn how to behave as individuals.

Whether considering homosexuality, drugs or kleptomania, all behavior is learned. We learn how to behave by our environmental orientation. However, we can also learn how to behave otherwise. That's why it is encouraging to see organizations who are actually helping people change aberrant lifestyle into new, more functional ones. There will always be a temperament (temptation), and there may always be conflict in our thinking process, but we can learn to behave in ways adaptive to our world and in keeping with Godly principles.

For years we have heard people state, "I'm a sanguine" or "I'm a choleric and that is why I'm so rude and self-centered, aggressive and mean." All people have basic tendencies and styles they have adapted towards living, but in civilized society, we must adopt what is healthful. Just because one has a certain temperament does not give them permission to act in ways destructive to others or one's self. We can and must learn to modify our predetermined desires for the betterment of all around us.

As it is with any kind of addiction, or emotional problem, the key to complete recovery is motivation or desire. If we do not desire to be different, no matter what happens to us, we probably will not be able to change. If an alcoholic has no motivation, or desire to be dry and sober, no matter what counseling techniques we use we probably will not be able to help them. If a drug addict does not see the need to be free from drugs, you can put him in jail but eventually he'll still get the drugs. There has to be a motivation or desire to be whole.

Behavior is learned through the environment, through our associations, beginning with our primary care givers at birth. In fact, we begin to learn even before birth. Research indicates that there are some things children learn which affect their personality even before they're born. Babies can even become addicted to drugs (crack babies) even in the womb.

If behavior is learned, then behavior can be unlearned. But there must first come the desire to change. We have to want our behavior changed. According to sociologists, people do what they do because they want to. They may say that they didn't want to do it. But they did have a choice. They didn't have to do whatever it is they did. A common Christian excuse is, "The devil made me do it," yet they are still in control over their actions. It can be argued logically that even if it was a demon that attempted to influence them, it was still up to them to yield to that demon in the first place. "The devil made me do it" has no basis for defense before God or the courts.

The question that must be asked is, "how do people become they way they are?" How do they become drug addicts? How do people become alcoholics? How do people become addicted to eating? Or become anorexic? Somehow the addiction occurred within their environment.

I'll give you a crude example through this little skit.

> Father: "If anybody touches my golf clubs I'll kill him. Let's get this straight. Those are mine and if anybody in this house touches those golf clubs, I swear, I'll kill him."

> (Now, he doesn't really mean that. He doesn't mean that he's literally going to kill somebody, but he wants to make his point in the strongest way he can make it.)

> So father comes home and discovers that his golf clubs have mysteriously been moved.

> Father: "Who moved my clubs? Johnny?"

> Johnny: "Not me."

(Johnny is not very old, but he's smart enough to know that he'll get killed if he says yes and he doesn't want to die.)

So Johnny lies. Are you following my reasoning? Where did Johnny learn that particular mask of "not me?" Johnny learned it through his environment. He was taught that the safest way to survive in this world is to admit nothing. Taken to an extreme, people can thus become pathological liars. They lie and lie and lie even when they don't need to. This is because they have learned that most of the time, if you're in trouble, you can get out of it by lying. If you practice lying all of the time, you'll avoid trouble.

How do people develop, for instance, the "I can't" mask? They hear people they trust say:

"Well, I can't do this right so I quit."

"I just can't do it."

"I've tried and I've tried but I can't do it."

Where did they learn this behavior? Which stage of development might this originate in? The stage of "Industry versus Shame and Guilt." This is where the parents said things like, "You can't do that. Oh well, let me do it for you."

The proper things for parents to say in this stage are similar to the following "You can do it Johnny. Go ahead, you can do it. Come on try." The problem is that Momma or This pattern is engraved in the child's mind. All children are highly impressionable. Thus, through repeated trials, where his efforts at autonomy are repeatedly thwarted, the child learns, "I can't." This creates a feeling of shame. He's ashamed because other kids can but he can't.

I remember a child in the fourth grade, a boy in my daughter's class. His mother brought him to school every day and met him every afternoon to take him home. I thought this was a little strange, especially since she only lived a few blocks away. All the other kids walked, but not him.

One day she came for a parent's conference and confided to the teacher, "I don't know what to do with him? I have to do everything for Kenny. He cannot do anything for himself. I can't even let him walk to school by himself. He'll get lost on the way school."

The teacher asked her an interesting question. "Have you ever let him try to walk to school by himself?"

"Oh no. I couldn't do that, he'd get lost."

"How do you know he would get lost? He's never been given the chance to try it. How do you know he can't find his to school? All he has to do is follow the other kids."

Here was a fourth grader who couldn't find his way to school, according to his mother. I suppose he'd probably been convinced of that. He's the kind of person that when grown would be constantly saying, "I can't do it." He'll no doubt choose to marry a woman who will do everything for him. People raised this way can learn to be dependent on someone else for their entire life, and many will turn to substances to deal with their sense of absolute inadequacy.

What about some of the other masks? How do they get there? How do people find themselves in situations where there is no ability to trust? They say, "I really need help but I do not know how to ask for it." (See Appendix Three: Stages of Development). It is in stage one that the child is totally dependent on other people. If mom, dad or some caregiver was not there to feed him, change his soiled diaper and generally take care of him, he would continue to reach out to his environment and those around him to meet his need, but it does not get met. Thus, as an adult the person will wonder if they ever do reach out to a counselor for help, will he or she get it?

This person has learned to mistrust; is unable to trust anybody.

When thinking about the masks or various defense mechanisms people use, the counselor will see how these fit into one of the categories of parental style that Erikson's research presents. The neglectful parenting style and the overprotective mother are two examples of these dysfunctional parental styles. Masks are simply a learned reaction to parenting.

How does an adult first learn to rationalize? First of all, an adult does not learn to rationalize. A child learns to rationalize, project, and repress. All of these defense mechanisms are learned as a result of parenting styles and specific activities that occur in their childhood environment. For instance, where does projection and the act of blaming others come from? There are always connections, which must be looked for and discovered when counseling. You must seek to discover:

Why did this person turn to drugs?

Why did this person, as a pre-teen, start drinking?

There must be a reason. Our desire is not just to get our clients off of their drug of choice. Our goal is to treat that which created the need, and then replacing the illegitimate methods of meeting needs with legitimate ones.

Self Image

One very pretty girl that I knew had a brother who attended our church. She wanted to be with the other kids, to be a part of the fellowship with other Christians. She tried so hard, but she was a teenage alcoholic. She was not only alcoholic, but she was an anorexic. This girl was quite beautiful except that she was extremely thin, though believing and stating that she was very fat.

No matter how thin an anorexic is, they always see themselves as fat. The only way this girl could deal with her emotional pain was to start drinking. When she drank she didn't feel the pain, thus leading to her alcoholism.

As hard as she tried to stop drinking, she couldn't break the addiction. She would not face the real problem. Because of her addiction, her self-image was distorted. However, telling her she was pretty, etc. would have been fruitless. Her response would have been outrage and anger. The counselor must help the client come to the conclusion that the way they see themselves is not an accurate depiction of how they truly are, but is distorted because of the substance they have been abusing. Most importantly, it is not the way God sees them, which is the way they really are.

12-step programs have helped thousands of people to gain freedom from alcohol. But to the AA member, are considered by the program to be an alcoholic for life, with no chance of redemption. They are told that they may not have had a drink for six years, but they are still an alcoholic, and must continue to go to the meetings on a regular basis to stay sober. Even after a long season of sobriety, they must stand and say, "Hi, my name is Joe, I'm an alcoholic." Every week they are confessing to what is in God's view, a lie. Even if they've been totally dry for years, they have to admit that they are still alcoholics.

The purpose for the extreme AA stance is to make a statement to the alcoholic that all they need to do is take one drink and they will relapse to full alcoholism. Research indicates that this is not true. However, it is true from a disease model that alcoholism can never be cured. Thus, once they buy into the AA philosophy, they will need the life long support of the group, the support of friends to remain abstinent from the use of alcohol. They never learn "self control" as a virtue, or moderation.

Since all behavior is learned, new behaviors must be learned to replace old, dysfunctional ones. Drinking or drugging behavior can be changed, the first step being to quit the drinking or drugging. However, the complexity of the disease/disorder requires a comprehensive approach, as presented throughout this book.

Chapter Six Questions for Discussion

1. In studying human development, what are the two views of learning?
2. Is all behavior learned?
3. What is the key to complete recovery?
4. Can behavior be unlearned?
5. How do people develop "I can't" mask?
6. Why does trust need to be established at the first stage of development?
7. Give two examples of dysfunctional parenting styles.

Chapter Seven

Co-Dependency

To gain a greater understanding of Co-dependency, we must first look at the concept of *intimacy*.

One of the greatest problems caused by drug and alcohol abuse is the collapse of intimacy. Many people start using drugs at pre-adolescent or adolescent age. At this age they are not yet ready for true intimacy. This causes their emotional development to be arrested at the developmental stage where they are ready for close friends and peer relationships, but they're not ready for intimacy.

Because their emotional development is arrested, when they reach 25 or 30 years old and get married they continue to respond at that emotionally immature pre-intimacy stage. According to Erickson's developmental theory, they are stuck in a stage of role-confusion. They do not know whether they are man or beast, a he-man or a wimp.

Many began drinking due to this role-confusion. Fear of facing adult responsibilities plague these individuals. The degree of role-confusion determines what developmental skills will be carried into marriage and determines their ability to experience true intimacy. Alcohol arrests the brain's functionality in the emotional realm, limiting growth. Thus the results are repeatedly broken marriages and many damaged lives.

A Problem With Intimacy

My friend Bob and his wife Luis lived in Denver for many years. We became very close. They had a young daughter about the same age as one of ours so we got together often. We met in church, quickly becoming fast friends.

As we got to know them, some of their problems began to surface. They had a tremendous problem with intimacy. It was particularly obvious. They talked very openly about it, which is in itself a little bizarre. One time, my friend Bob said, "You know, it's getting to point where my wife doesn't want to have sex anymore."

She had stated, "Alright, alright. If that's all you want is sex, sex, sex, that's okay, you just put your 2 dollars on the night table and you can have your sex."

He said, "I can go to Mexico and get better for 2 dollars."

It is a wonder they didn't kill each other that night!

Since we were friends we did not feel able to objectively counsel with them, so we referred them to a colleague of ours in the city. The full story, as told by Bob and Louis, came to us after their counseling.

Bob was a young man with certain problems related to his childhood who had married a woman with other problems stemming from her childhood. Because of this, they were both unable to be intimate. He wasn't really interested in intimacy. He was interested in personal sexual fulfillment. And she wasn't interested in that because she didn't know how to enjoy herself sexually. She took no pleasure in it whatsoever!

To complicate matters, Bob would come home late from work, having first stopped at a local pub to bolster his "courage" to face Louis. She also began to consume large quantities of wine, creating an explosive and unhappy situation. The alcohol, which infinitely "assisted" their intimacy (she was able to get in the mood) grew instead into a barrier of safety to hide behind, adding insult to injury.

What a sad situation! Of course, sex is not the totality of intimacy. However, it is one important part of a covenantal marital relationship (see 1 Corinthians 7).

There are people that for some reason or another are unable to have an ongoing sexual relationship, but they can still have an intimate relationship. They're still close. They want to be together. They don not know how to share life together.

Lack of Intimacy — Dependency — Co-Dependency

There are many people abusing chemical substances of various kinds living with someone else that neither understands abuse, or has become what is termed an "enabler" or "co-dependent." The "enabler" also has a need to continue rescuing the addict which is met through helping or attempting to meet the needs of the alcoholic.

An enabler does not really want the addict to fully recover... That would make the enabler feel useless or not wanted. Often enablers and co-dependents need to have an addict "to help" so badly they may even sabotage any attempt at a full recovery! They have a real need or "addiction to help and rescue scenarios."

There is a great difference between dependency and intimacy. Some people become extremely dependent on their spouse and mistake that for intimacy. Dependency is entirely different from intimacy. Dependency says, "I love you because I need you to fill the void in my life. Without you I would be absolutely nothing. My whole self-image, my whole sense of who I am depends on you."

This creates a situation such as when the husband dies suddenly or leaves the home, the woman falls completely apart. In other cases she might immediately marry somebody that was just like the husband that died.

In codependency syndrome, this can become an extremely vicious cycle. A woman will be married to an alcoholic who may beat her, the kids, and spend all of his money on his drink. She suffers for several years with this alcoholic until finally, with great courage, she divorces him once and for all.

Then what does she do? She soon marries another alcoholic similar to the one she just lost, and the cycle begins all over again. Why?

Her purpose in life is to protect and mother. The greatest thrill in life she gets is, "I'm going to help fix this man." Usually, the woman will not admit that the husband is an alcoholic. She'll protect him. "Oh, well, you know he takes a few drinks, but hey, I know people who are much, much worse." This type of woman will rationalize to be able to work her "project."

A very close friend of one of my colleagues had a heart problem. My colleague and he had met in re-hab. They became good friends. The man had a second wife. One day he told his story, which was a classic case of co-dependency. The man was an alcoholic who one day decided, through alcoholics anonymous, to stop. He went to AA, quit drinking and his wife, who had nagged him for years to quit drinking, suddenly decided to divorce him. She knew how to live with an alcoholic, but did not know how to live with a man who was sober.

There was a symbiotic need being met in this relationship. The wife had "permission" to nag at her husband over his addiction, and the husband had "permission" to get drunk because his wife was such a rotten nag. When one half of the cycle was broken, the rationalizations for the dysfunctional behavior were also broken, which caused a collapse of the entire relationship.

When a spouse is an "enabler," they have a deep need to take care of the alcoholic. When the spouse finally becomes drug or alcohol free, the homeostatic balance or equilibrium in the relationship is upset. At that point, the enabling spouse no longer has a need for the relationship and may choose to get out to find another "sick, needy" person to "help." This is a classic occurrence, happening only too frequently.

Freedom!!!

One of the many goals of treatment is to establish freedom. Freedom cannot be gained until a person has learned to take responsibility for their own life. As long as someone else is taking care of them and their problems, they will never be able to take responsibility for themselves and thus be free.

You've certainly heard the unbelievable horror stories of fathers who have sexually abused their children, and mothers who made excuses, covering up the behavior, protecting the father. I have heard mothers telling the children, "Well, you mustn't tell anybody because if you do, they'll take daddy away and we won't have a daddy." This is the height of self-centered co-dependency. Lives are ruined because of codependent "enablers" who allow the deviant to continue the destructive behavior.

In counseling co-dependents, the goal is empowerment, through modeling and teaching assertive, responsible behavior with origins in corrected thinking.

The process must begin with changing their dependent thought and behavior patterns to independent ones. ones. The next step in achieving a level of normalcy involves moving the now "independent" former "addict" and "codependent" into a state of "interdependence." Interdependent behavior is the long term goal of the counseling process.

Chapter Seven Questions for Discussion

1. How does role confusion affect intimacy?
2. What is dependency versus intimacy?
3. Explain dependency.
4. What is an "enabler" ?
5. When can freedom be obtained?
6. What is the goal when counseling co-dependents?

Chapter Eight

Treatment

Without a proper *assessment*, appropriate treatment is not possible. Our initial assessment or data gathering on a client should include several components[7]. They include personal and family history, a genogram of sorts (multi-generational history), assessment of drinking/drug behavior, effects of use/abuse in key life arenas, essential temperament/personality profile etc. The more thorough the assessment, the more concise the treatment plan and the more potentially efficacious the treatment protocol.

After the assessment, the counselor must determine a plan of action for the client. At the risk of being redundant, it is vital to remember that the number one requirement for any treatment is motivation. You have to know if the individual is motivated to make change. Is the client motivated to make the initial change of stopping their drinking, drugging behaviors. This is the first and most important step. Without quitting, little else can be accomplished. You must have a strategy for this first.

Motivation

There are many levels of *motivation*. What type of motivation may cause a person to seek professional help?

One motivation for a substance abuser is the loss of family. The wife says, "That's it. I've had it. I'm leaving and I'm taking the kids." Or, "Get out you dirty bum, and take your junk with you." Losing one's family can be a strong motivation, driving some people to seek help. The abuser, who often lives in the stupor of denial, may respond, "Oh, I didn't know that it was that bad. I bring the check home, and feed you, and give you good clothes, and I take care of you. I didn't even know we had a problem here." They are often oblivious to how difficult life has become for their spouse and children.

Loss of health is another major motivator. When the substance abuser goes to the doctor and he is told, "You have sclerosis of the liver. You have

---

[7] For more on assessment, see *Assessment of Human Needs*, by DeKoven.

approximately a year to live if you don't stop drinking today." That's motivation!

When the doctor says, "You have diabetes. You have got to cut out all of the sugars, count your calories, take in no alcohol whatsoever, or you are going to go blind first, and then you will die of a heart attack shortly thereafter... that is, if your feet do not get gangrene and fall off first."

Many people lose their job because they can't function with their addicted lifestyle. Many abusers are forced into treatment for emotional problems which are substance-abuse related. The boss says, "You just can't get along with your co-workers. You're missing too many days from work." Or, "We're going to have to let you go unless you get some serious help."

The legal system provides another form of motivation. When the judge says, "Either you go for professional substance abuse counseling or you go to jail," an addict will generally choose the counseling, even though they don't want to be in counseling ("I don't need it"). This provides quite a "hook" for the counselor! "Do you really want to get better?" the counselor states.

To this the client replies, "No, but I don't want to go to jail either!"

So the counselor has the power to say, "Okay. If you miss one appointment, or are late even one time, I will call your probation officer and you're off to jail." Thus, the outside reinforcement (carrot on stick) can be helpful in keeping the counselee engaged in the treatment process.

The average substance abuser has a great fear of shameful exposure, loss of relationship, rejection and abandonment. These are the frequent results of their alcoholic/drug abusive lifestyle. The fear of loss is a motivator, and is a force driving them to their avoidant escapist behavior. Thus, sensitivity and balance must be exercised by the counselor. Too much pressure may drive them towards their substance of choice, too little pressure gives them easy escape.

Motivation for some addicts to seek treatment can be loss of control. Here the abuser realizes that, "I'm very fortunate that I didn't hurt somebody this last time. I could have killed somebody." Though not as strong a motivation as some of the others, it can be a powerful motivation when a person finally wakes up and says, "What's wrong with me? What I'm doing is stupid. Why am I doing this? I'm hurting my family, I'm hurting everybody else. I'm getting some help!"

This would be a very positive, if not transient, motivation in and of itself. The stronger the motivation, the greater the possibility for the ultimate success of the treatment program.

Sometimes grief over the loss of a loved one through death will drive a person to irresponsible behavior. They may state, "I really blew it. The one thing that my mother wanted was to see me clean and sober, going to church and serving the Lord; and now, she's gone."

Another motivation could be the fear of losing fellowship with a body of believers. If an addict were a part of a community of Christians, this person would say to himself, "I really don't want to lose my fellowship because this is the greatest thing I have ever been involved with... much bigger than my addiction!"

Losing a great Christian fellowship through substance abuse is much the same as losing one's natural family. If family is important to the abuser, fear of loss could be a strong motivator. Of course, the strength of family motivation depends on the quality of the relationships, and the strength of family ties.

There are probably many other motivations that could be mentioned. These are the most common. Some may be stronger than others. Of all of these, the strongest motivation will be whichever one springs from a personal decision made by the client. The client must truly want to change to see any long term results.

Even the forced choice of jail or counseling, though an initially strong motivation, does not mean that the person will want to personally make long term changes. Their denial, or inability to see the severity of their problem can keep them from ultimate change. As the counselor, you must help your client see his or her destructive patterns. You must confront your client to face the facts. However, the motivation to change will itself change over time, often in response to a strong, consistent, therapeutic relationship.

Your Relation With The Client

The counselor's relationship with the client is quite likely the most important part of the counseling process. If the client believes that the counselor is looking down on him, is judgmental or lacks understanding, the process can be thwarted. Some of us who counsel have our own issues to face. Some counselors come from an alcoholic family. If as a child, the counselor has lived with and was raised by alcoholic, abusive parents, there could likely be negative feelings about alcoholism and alcoholics.

If that's true then you need to work out your own issues before you enter the counseling field. As the old adage states, "Physician, heal thyself!" There is nothing that an alcoholic discerns faster than the realization that you do not approve of him or her in light of their problem.

When an alcoholic announces or acknowledges, "I'm an alcoholic," The counselor must assume that behind the alcoholism is a person of worth. It is the addiction to the alcohol or substance that is making him or her less than God's intention.

If a counselor allows himself to feel, "He's just like that drunken old man of mine," or "He's just like my drunken mother," they will not be able to help the hurting addict.

Thus, as counselor, one must win the client's acceptance of his role as counselor. Of course, that's true with all of counseling, but especially when counseling men and women suffering from the cruel bondage of substance abuse.

A wise counselor must look at their own attitude before embarking on the journey of healing.

Our attitudes toward the hurting must be therapeutic, which includes having empathy (feeling with them, identifying with their suffering), warmth (being accepting of their personage, not necessarily their behavior) and respect (viewing them as a unique creation of God who is in need of redirection, grace and instruction).

The Bible states we are to guard our hearts or set a watch over it. We must, as counselors, set aside our personal agendas for the sake of the client, and allow the love of Christ to be our prime motivation for ministry to the client.

A Support Group?

One portion of a dynamic treatment program for the substance abuser is the support group. This can be a combination of *AA*, *NAS* or *ACA* group meeting weekly or more often as well as home fellowships. These fellowship groups are not therapy groups per se, but self-help meetings where men and women with common maladies assist one another.

Addicts may support one another because of empathy or feeling of, "I know exactly where you're at. I know where you're coming from. I've been there and I know what you're dealing with; I can help you deal with this particular aspect of your problem and then, you can help me." AA and the 12 step group have been highly successful with thousands of people.

Their success is due to the fact that most of the people that attend are recovering alcoholics. It is easier for a fellow alcoholic to say, "I know where you're coming from."

If you're a person raised in Sunday school having never had a drink, and won't even take medicine with alcohol in it, when somebody says, "I'm an alcoholic," you cannot say, "I know what you're going through."

The fact is, we have no idea what their going through. You may still be able to counsel them but not with the highest level of empathy. Unless you've "been there" don't pretend that you have. They can see right through that.

This does not mean you must become a substance abuser to counsel one. However, those that have recovered from the slavery of substance abuse have an advantage over those that have never been addicted. One advantage is that they know how strong the temptation or grip of sin that substance have. Secondly, they can spot a con from a hundred yards away.

Watch The Con

One of the characteristics of addictive people is their ability to cons others. If you've ever been in a close relationship with an active substance abuser you have probably been taken in. They tell lies that they believe themselves. They can con a naïve counselor, making us believe that the moon is the sun and the sun is the moon. This lying, manipulative behavior is a result of the alcoholic/drug addictive behavior.

However, especially in the early stage of recovery, the counselor must be careful. If we are not aware of the dynamics when beginning to counsel with a counselee who is dealing with issues of substance abuse, they can con us with sob stories of their unfortunate plight. They know, for instance, that the counselor's recommendation is going to keep them out of jail (or allow them to return home…). After a certain amount of treatment, the report we write to the probation department is the thing that is going to get them off the hook. Thus, they will play all of the games.

They will weep and cry real tears, because the con cons himself until he really believes he means it.

"I will do anything. I just want to get help, I want to get out of this mess I'm in," and on and on they go.

If we are not careful we can become codependent or enablers ourselves. "Oh you poor person. I know, oh it's so terrible." It is essential to remain clinically objective, not allowing the client's problems to become yours. Stories told by the client must be verified and our counseling must remain focused on sobriety, which includes remaining substance free and being in their right mind.

Treatment Plans

Assuming that the client has proper motivation for change, and some form of sincere desire on the part of the individual, there are various treatment modalities available to us. The two primary models are the Medical and Psychosocial.

The medical model is just that: a way of dealing with addiction by the use of medication and/or by providing treatment within a medical facility. All treatments will begin with detoxification.

With some programs such as "Teen Challenge", a detox program may mean to quit "cold turkey". This means that a counselor stays with the addict as they sweat, go into convulsions, and throw up. During this process, the partner stays with them while the poison works its way out of the abuser's body.

Detoxification simply means the removal of toxins or poisons out of the system. Detoxification from the substance is needed prior to further treatment.

There will always be some pain associated with detox. However, detoxification must occur if there is going to be any possible hope for change.

Cold Turkey Is Not Always The Way To Go

In extreme cases, or when the client's health isn't conducive for the "cold turkey" approach, the counselor may have to be creative with the detox process. For example, if the person has a severe heart problem, detox must occur gradually. Though it is commonly believed that the pain of detox is therapeutic, recent studies indicate that controlled detoxification, under medial supervision is the most effective, and certainly the most humane. The only lesson learned from "cold turkey" detox is that it is painful, and to be avoided.

My dear friend and associate Dr. Bohac relates a tragic story:

"I lost a very close friend a couple years ago. He was a life long alcoholic. I had never, in all the years that I knew him, seen him drunk. But he drank at least one fifth of either vodka or scotch every day. We spent a whole month in Europe, Ireland and England together. I observed him buy and drink a fifth of whiskey every day, but I never once saw him drunk. He was a classic alcoholic. He never passed out, he never staggered and you could talk to him and never know that he was drunk. You'd smell it on his breath, and just assume that he'd been drinking.

"The fact is the drinking was taking its toll on him physically. His internal organs were suffering the consequences of continuous alcohol addiction. The liver can only process so much poison before it begins to break down, and sooner or later sclerosis of the liver will develop. That's what he had.

"When we returned from Ireland, he was very sick. One night, he was very sick, so he called a doctor. He and his wife did not have a regular doctor, because the first thing the doctor would say is, "get off of the alcohol." So why go to the doctor—He just wants to take away my drink. However, due to his physical pain and distress, he called the doctor who determined he needed immediate hospitalization.

"The doctor was determined to detox this life long alcoholic cold turkey. He was in excruciating, horrible, and dehumanizing pain. Some people might say, "well, you've got to get him detoxed." Well in this case, the man died a couple of weeks later. The pain of the detox process combined with the deterioration of his bodily systems was too much for my friend to take.

It was inevitable that my friend was going to die. He was in terrible shape. However, he did not have to die so soon. Nor in such agonizing pain. With proper care his life could have been extended and his end made peaceful."

Thank God there are humane ways to detox a patient. One way is the usage of medication. For example, Methadon is a synthetic substitute for heroin which does not have the physically addicting qualities of heroin. It can still be psychologically addicting, but does not cause the physical damage that heroin does. It's a second rate substitute for getting high from heroin, but with some people it works. Getting them off the heroin, off the street, can be a first step towards their ultimate freedom.

Another drug used to ease the pain of detox is Valium. Valium can be highly addictive when taken in large doses, but it can calm the body from the intense reaction caused by detox. It must be used under medical supervision, and is designed for short-term usage.

What Do We Do After Detox?

A hospital based program is one option. Most large hospitals have a detox center and a 28 day program designed to start the patient on a life of sobriety. The 28 day program (28 days because insurance companies will pay for that length of time) is not sufficient to cause a cure. It is a beginning.

Many people who have become clean during the 28 day period, are able stay clean from then on. Once the poison was out of their system they were able to make decisions for permanent change. Once they began to feel better they realized, "I didn't know how rotten I really felt." They begin to fight against the temptations, develop necessary support systems, and move on with their life.

Fourteen days after a hospitalization ends there is a recommended 6 month follow-up in AA or NA[8]. Some counselors might choose to add group counseling as an adjunct to 12 step programs and family therapy can often be helpful once sobriety has been chosen. Relapse prevention is one of the major goals of after care.

For very long term addicts, a residential program where individuals are put into a residence that is much closer to the pattern of living in a family as opposed to a hospital is recommended. The Teen Challenge program is an example of such a program. In a residential program, patients live together 24 hours a day with people of like affliction. This program has proven to be highly successful with motivated clients.

Long term programs are not always successful. A reason for some to drop out, is that they are also addicted to nicotine and they smoke. When a person enters a Christian home, smoking is often prohibited. Many clients

---

[8] For a complete 12 step program from a Christian perspective, see *12 Step to Wholeness*, by DeKoven.

cannot handle this added stress. They can beat drugs easier than they can smoking. Some will leave a program because they can't quit smoking.

Another reason that some leave is because of the high emphasis on religion; especially Christianity. When enrolled in Christian program,[9] they are bombarded with religion as a primary solution. Some cannot handle this emphasis because they are not emotionally prepared for the intensity of religious fervor.

Psychological Treatment

Another mode of treatment is psychological, which is less effective than the medical model. This is due to a lack of client motivation, and the result of denial caused by addictive behavior. A psychologist or counselor can only help a person as far as the person wants to be helped. As stated previously, if they lack motivation to change, and remain actively addicted, there is little that a counselor can do to help.

Once a person is clean and moving towards sobriety psychological help or Christian counseling can be helpful.

As a Christian counselor, there are several therapies that can be effective. Of course, you will need to mix and match them to your own personal taste, but you should achieve fairly good results. There are a few different therapies which have been tried to varying degrees of success. The second half of this book describes in detail their theory, practice and etiology. Also, provided are further insight and references which will act as a springboard for greater success of your own counseling methodology.

The three most common are:

Cognitive Behavior Therapy

Reality Therapy

Insight Therapy

Remember, no therapy will be effective until the person is clean, but each of these therapies attempts to help the client face their problem from the perspective of reality. Most abusers have a very poor image of themselves, a predominant reason for hiding behind their "masks." The counselor's

---

[9] This would also be true for other non-clinical programs such as Victory Outreach.

role is to assist them to see that below the rottenness caused by substance abuse is a good person worth opportunity to succeed in life.

With both Cognitive Behavioral Treatment and Reality Therapy, the goal is to help the client look at their situation from a healthier perspective. "Look, you're going to lose you're home. You've already lost your car. Your family is moving out on you. You've lost your job. Take a solid look at the direction you're going. Where are you going to be 6 months from now? Probably in the morgue or laying someplace in a gutter dying from this substance." The hope is that this reality approach will stir them to positive action.

With the Cognitive Behavioral approach, the desire is to help the client confront the wrong beliefs and behaviors as truth. Though the substance abuser may feel he or she cannot change or handle certain situations, can never make amends or are hopeless, the truth is different depending on perspective and choices.

A Reality Therapy orientation adds a "Contract for Change," holding the client responsible for choices without condemnation or criticism. The focus of each approach is to reorient the thinking of the client, similar to renewing the mind, and encouraging them to make new, healthier choices.

The least effective treatment is the Insight Therapies. This is due to the fact that insight is rarely sufficient to bring change to behavior disorders. Knowing why someone does drugs may only give additional excuses to remain a victim of their own choices (the all too common, "My mother made me do it!").

Family Therapy

Another therapeutic approach to the treatment of substance abuse is family therapy. Most family treatment begins with intervention. This form of treatment can be very effective, especially because it not only helps the addict, but it also helps the enablers in the family. Most of the time, when there is drug abuse within a family, the whole family suffers dysfunction. The substance abuser itself causes relational problems between the members of the family.

Family intervention will usually include "tough love". Tough love is demonstrated through actions that say, "The destructive behavior will stop. . . . OR else." Family interventions must be well coordinated to be effective, lead by a specialist, as been discussed previously in this book. Family Therapy continues after the substance abuser is in treatment, to help the family cope and prepare for the future.

Intervention

One treatment program that effectively uses Intervention is the Betty Ford Clinic. Some of the most popular people in the political and entertainment business have been helped at Betty Ford because of the intervention of a family. Betty Ford entered treatment in a similar fashion. Her family set her down one day and said, "That's it. You're an alcoholic and we're cutting you off. You're out. We're done with you. We'll have nothing to do with you anymore unless you get help, right now!" Intervention worked for Betty Ford, and her successful treatment resulted in the development of her now famous clinic.

Most likely the best combination of treatments for a functional abuser of substances (one who is able to work, etc.) is a twenty-eight day in-patient treatment program, begun by family intervention, followed by a 6 Month AA/NA program with Family Therapy for support of sobriety.

Where insurance does not allow the twenty-eight day program, and the client is well motivated, a intensive day treatment can jolt them to effective action. This would also be followed by a six month AA/NA program with family treatment, which is Cognitive Behavioral/Reality Therapy oriented. These two therapies are the most effective for both becoming clean and sober, and also prevention of further usage (relapse).

Spiritual Treatment

The spiritual approach is one quite familiar to Christians. The Supernatural power of Christ is not only to be used to help addicts to admit they need the Lord, of course, that's only the beginning. The client will need longer care, and local churches can develop good counseling programs where individuals can grow into wholeness over time.

Sadly, many churches naively assume that when a person becomes born again they will behave like a full fledged, mature Christian. Like all other converts, they are just babies in Christ. It does not matter their age. They may be forty years old, but when they come to the altar they're a new born babe, needing milk from the Word for nourishment. They need help and care.

We would never take a new born child from the hospital, swat him on the backside and say, "You're on your own Sonny," and send him out the door. Yet we do that very thing in the spiritual realm. When someone first comes to Christ, they are starting from square one in their spiritual growth. Even if the new convert has studied scripture all of his life it doesn't matter. In Christ they were made alive. They could not make sense of what the scriptures were saying prior to their spiritual birth. It is impossible to understand the things of God until first converted.

From the moment of conversion, a spiritual journey begins. We must learn our alphabet before we begin to form words. The learning curve begins, and teaching to bring character can only be done within a nurturing environment. This does not mean that the new convert is to simply come to church, clap their hands and get happy when they are singing. Nurturing is an entirely different thing. Nurturing is taking personal care of an individual for their growth.

Rarely does immediate transformation occur from an initial spiritual experience. Yet, even when deliverance from substance abuse does occur as a result of giving one's life to Christ, there remains the hard work of sanctification. This is the continuous work of the Holy Spirit on a yielded heart, which is the result of discipline, of the Christian walk, God's Word, prayer, worship and obedience.

They Have To Submit

The first step in change of any kind is to **admit** to a problem. Following this, the client must be willing to **submit** to a process of change. There is brokenness that must take place, where men and women are willing to not only get help and listen, but then to **commit** to authoritative care in their life. This is to be done within the framework of the church and is the reason the church needs mature men and women as caregivers.

The church is the Lord's healing laboratory, the place where He conducts His "grand experiment," the transformation of lives. Clients need to become a part of an active fellowship. They must submit to elders of a church and be willing to listen to mature believers. All believers need correction, to grow up.

It can be difficult to pastor people emerging from drug abuse or alcoholism. Some of these young, brand new Christians come from a highly dysfunctional lifestyle. They may not want to listen to the leaders or counselors. They do not readily accept input to their lives. At first they may seem compliant, but after a while, they begin to rebel[10]. They may leave the church and find a fellowship where people will not tell them what to do.

We must remind ourselves that the great goal for all people is salvation, transformation and complete healing. The goal of Christian Counseling is the healing of the whole person. This takes time, patience, skill and a willingness to walk through the "Valley of the Shadow of Death" for God's wounded.

Always Remember This:

Don't put a bandage over a splinter. Take the splinter out. It may hurt when taking it out, but it must come out.

Clean out the wound, put in the antiseptic, dress it properly, and do everything you can to effect healing.

The same concept applies to all ministry. Total ministry means healing from salvation to glorification.

---

[10] This is caused by the substance abuse itself, and rarely is a "Spirit of Rebellion." Remember, their maturation was arrested in teen years [for most]. Recovery will help them to grow through those arrested stages.

Chapter Eight Questions for Discussion

1. What might motivate a person to seek help?

2. Explain why it is important for a counselor to win the client's acceptance.

3. What is meant by a "con artist?"

4. Explain the two primary models of treatment.

5. Describe a standard treatment regimen.

6. What can be done to prevent relapse?

7. Name the three most common therapies.

8. Why are submission and intervention important in the treatment process?

Part 2

Theory and Practice

Chapter Nine

Drugs Of Abuse

There are many different kinds of drugs which can be abused, from carpet cleaners, to heroin sold on corners, to prescriptions handed over the pharmacy counter, to the cigarettes bought at the gas station. Drugs are all around, and though they all have an effect on the human body, mind and spirit, all behave in different ways... some more fiendish than others.

In this chapter we explore the most common substances abused today. From alcohol to street drugs to club drugs, the primary substances abused are cataloged for a better understanding. Information is power.

ALCOHOL

Classification:	Depressant, sedative hypnotic
Type:	Legal and Illegal
Common chemical substances:	Ethanol or ethyl alcohol. Other forms of alcohol are much more toxic to the body, and are rarely used.

Commonly available forms:	Type	Average % of alcohol
	Beer	3-6% (6-12 proof)
	Table Wine	11-15% (22-30 proof)
	Fortified Wine	20% (40 proof)
	Liqueur	25-35% (50-70% proof)
	Liquor	40-50% (40-100 proof)
	Pure Alcohol	95% (190 proof)

Effects and Precautions:

In small amounts alcohol produces a sense of calmness which relaxes the muscles. In larger doses, this drug adversely affects the brain causing slurred speech, poor coordination and poor judgment. Alcohol also produces slow and uncertain reflexes. The user loses control over their own body.

The signs of overdose, or drunkenness, are the smell of alcohol and the obvious displays of intoxication. During an overdose, an intoxicated person may experience hallucinations. These may occur on any one of the following four senses: sight, smell, touch and hearing. Fortunately for the drinker, they are usually so intoxicated that these images do not disturb them.

Some of the damage of alcohol abuse include amnesia, permanent memory loss, and danger to the cerebellum. Alcohol abusers can permanently destroy portions of their brain, resulting in loss of balance and coordination. The optic nerves are often affected with blurred and dim vision. The G.I. tract receives the brunt of the assault from alcohol. Ulcers often form due to drinking. Cirrhosis of the liver, or scarring, and Pancreatitis are the more fatal affects of alcoholism. This usually occurs after years of abuse.

Withdrawal from alcohol can be dangerous, but rarely is it fatal. Under the supervision of a doctor, the chances of death are even more rare. During withdrawal, it is common to experience anxiety, irritability, weakness, a loss of appetite, shakes, insomnia and seizures. These usually occur within 24-48 hours of the final drink. As these occur, it is always best to have a doctor's care.

Antidepressants

Classification:	Psycho-Active, anti-psychotic
Type:	Legal By Prescription
Common chemical substances:	Tricyclic antidepressants, Tetracyclics, MAO Inhibitors, Lithium
Methods of abuse:	Most commonly, these are taken orally, but they can be injected.

Commonly available forms:	Name	Chemical
	Tofranil	Imipromine
	Elavil	Amitriptyline
	Aventyl	Nortriptyline
	Vivactil	Protriptyline
	Perfofrane/Norpramine	Desopramine

101

Sinequan	Doxepin
Ludiomil	Maprotiline
Marplan	Isocarboxazid
Nardil	Phenelzine
Lithium	

Effects and Precautions:

The effect of an antidepressant is gradual. In some cases, it may take 3 to 4 weeks for the drug to take effect. The role of these drugs is to relieve deep depression from anxiety and other sources. Some of these drugs (namely Elavil and Sinequan) have a sedating affect which occurs immediately, in many cases relieving insomnia. Some of the negative affects of using these drugs include dry mouth, blurred vision and difficulty urinating.

These drugs do not produce a physical dependency, and can be discontinued with little or no discomfort. There is little potential for abuse, though many drug abusers (mainly heroin abusers) like the effects. Some sources suggest that this is due to a deeper psychological depression, not necessarily related to their drug addiction.

These drugs are rarely overdosed on for the sake of getting high. They have been used in suicide attempts. The affects of an overdose can be fatal and immediate hospital care is required.

Barbiturates

Classification:	Depressant, sedative hypnotic
Street Slang:	"Barbs" and "Downers"
Type:	Synthetic legal and illegal
Common chemical substances:	Amobarbital (amytal), Pentabarbital (nembutal) and Secobarbital (seconal).
Methods of abuse:	These drugs are taken orally

Effects and Precautions:

Very much like alcohol, this class of drug, taken in small amounts produces a sort of calmness and relaxes the muscles. In somewhat larger doses, this drug can cause slurred speech, a staggering gait, poor judgment and slow, uncertain reflexes.

Barbiturate overdose is a factor in nearly one-third of all reported drug-related deaths. An amazing statistic! These include suicides and accidental overdoses. Because of the way it fogs the mind, a user may take one dose, become confused and unintentionally take additional and perhaps larger doses. In an overdose, or when taken with other drugs like alcohol, death may come due to depression of the respiratory center in the brain.

On the street, these drugs are often used in combination with stimulants, such as cocaine, amphetamines and crystal meth an amphetamine. In medical practice, barbiturates are used to treat epilepsy. These are also used as an anti-anxiety agent, as a sedative while treating patients experiencing withdrawal from alcohol, heroin and other stimulants. Barbiturates are most dangerous when combined with alcohol.

While withdrawing from this drug, it is quite common to experience tremors, elevated blood pressure and pulse, sweating, and possible seizures. Withdrawal can be life threatening, necessitating medical care!

Hallucinogens

Classification:	Hallucinogens	
Type:	Synthetic and Natural	
Common chemical substances:	LSD, PCP, Belladonna	
Methods of abuse:	Swallowed, injected, snorted…	
Different Chemicals:	Name	Chemical
	LSD	Lysergic Acid Diethylamide
	Psilocybin	Source: Mexican Mushroom
	Mescaline	Source: cactus plant
	THC	Tetrahydrocannabinol
	Morning Glory	
	Nutmeg	Myristicin
	STP	
	DMT	Dimethyltryptamine
	Belladonna	
	Alkaloids	Methapyrilene
	PCP	Phenyclidine
	Peyote	
	Yohimbine	

MDA   Methylene
                       Dioxyamphetamine
       Khat

Effects and Precautions:

These drugs are used for three reasons. Their primary use is to achieve an altered state of awareness. Those who take this drug generally desire to have hallucinations. The second reason is for the sense of Euphoria it produces. The third reason is religious. Peyote is the only one of these drugs which is legal for public use. The Native American Church takes this hallucinogen at its meetings.

One of the clinical symptoms of using a hallucinogen is an altered perception. It is not unusual for users to experience what is known as sensory pathway crossover (synesthesia). This means that the user can perhaps hear colors, taste sounds, or see touch. Hallucinations may occur in any of the five senses. In addition to these symptoms, there is also increased awareness with a loss of control.

Users will often become deluded, becoming more susceptible to suggestion. This can often lead to violence. As with other drugs, the pupils may become dilated, the pulse rate may elevate and the user may experience some loss of psychomotor coordination. There is often a clouding of thought processes and muscle tremors as well.

When working with an individual who is under the influence, there are certain measures you should take to help. First, make sure to provide emotional support. Put them in a calm environment, focusing on relief of anxiety. Remember never to leave the patient alone. It is not unusual for a hallucinogenic drug user to walk out a window, thinking it is a doorway, or into traffic, not noticing the cars whizzing by. As you help the user, make sure to give verbal support. Encourage them to take their experience a moment at a time, to maintain some sense of control over the experience.

Special notes for handling PCP users is not to ever attempt painful methods of restraint (this includes arm locks, holding their necks and so on). Since PCP is an analgesic, the intoxicated person may resist, not feeling the pain, to the point of great physical harm to both them and the one restraining them. Users have suffered broken bones and in some cases died trying to escape from their restrainers.

Also of note is the fact that PCP is fat soluble. This means that a user takes the drug and it is absorbed by the body's fat cells. This can result in later intoxication, even without the presence of the drug. To rid the body of PCP, a few glasses of cranberry juice a day can add acid to the urine and blood, thus dissolving the PCP and passing it out of the body through the urine.

Luckily, there are no real affects of withdrawal accompanying these drugs. There is the occasional flashback, and depression has been reported after discontinuing use. A theory suggests that this may be due to the way some hallucinogens are similar to amphetamines. However, the actual source for the depression is not conclusively known.

Marijuana

Classification:	Cannabinols
Type:	Illegal
Common chemical substances:	Made from cannabis sativa plant
Methods of abuse:	Smoked or swallowed

Effects and Precautions:

Marijuana and its counterpart Hashish (marijuana having a higher level of tetrahydrocannabinol) are widely used throughout the United States for four reasons: recreation, a sense of euphoria, perceptual intensification and peer pressure. Peer pressure is how most abusers get started on the drug.

The symptoms of marijuana use include an elevated pulse, dry mouth, bloodshot eyes, allergic reactions, obvious signs of intoxication, slowed reflexes, impaired ability to learn and an increase in appetite. In very rare cases, adverse reactions such as panic and depression may follow marijuana use. Hormonal changes have also been noted, lowering the immune system and testosterone levels in men. Overdose is uncommon, but the "high" may last 12-48 hours.

Minor Tranquilizers

Classification:	Depressant, sedative
Type:	Legal By Prescription and Over the Counter
Common chemical substances:	Benzodiazepines, Meprobamate, antihistamines (which actually have a

	low abuse potential)	
Methods of abuse:	Most commonly, these are taken orally, but in rare cases they can be injected.	
Different Chemicals:	Name	Chemical
	Valium	Diazepam
	Librium	Chlordiazepoxide
	Serax	Oxazepam
	Tranxine	Chlorazepate
	Ativan	Lorazepam
	Equinil	
	Miltown	
	Atarax, Vistaril	Hydroxyzine
	Benadryl	Diphenhydramine
	Dormin, Nytol, etc.	Methapyrilene

Effects and Precautions:

These drugs are generally less destructive than their alcohol and barbiturates counterparts. Minor tranquilizers generally do not cloud one's consciousness, or impair coordination as other drugs. With this drug comes a sense of calmness and relief of anxiety. These drugs relieve nausea and other problems stemming from gastrointestinal disorders.

The main problem with tranquilizers as it relates to overdose is that they are rarely taken alone. More often than not, a drug like valium is taken with alcohol, producing potentially fatal results. When a person overdoses on a mild sedative, without the involvement of other drugs, side effects similar to neurological disease may occur. When these symptoms are present, all use of the drug should be discontinued.

Withdrawal from these drugs can be difficult. The process usually goes quickly. Many people who have become physically dependent on Minor Tranquilizers do not know it. They may experience insomnia, irritability, restlessness and aches, never making the connection. On occasion, while going through withdrawal from these drugs, an individual may experience a seizure. This is rare and often catches the drug user off guard.

Narcotics and Opiates

Classification:	Narcotics	
Type:	Legal by prescription and Illegal	
Common chemical substances:	Opium, Morphine, others	
Methods of abuse:	Oral Ingestion, Inhaling or by Injection into the Muscles and Veins	
Commonly available forms:	Name	Chemical
	Opium	Derived from the poppy
	Morphine	Made of 10% raw opium
	Codeine	Made of 5% raw opium
	Heroin*	Diacetyl Morphine
	Dilaudid*	Hydromorphone
	Numorphan*	Oxymorphone
	Percodan*	Oxycodone
	Levo-Dromoran**	Levorphanol
	Dolphine**	Methodone
	Demerol**	Meperidine
	Darvon**	Propoxyphene
	LAAM**	Levo-alpha-acetylmethodol

* derivative of Morphine
** all synthetic narcotic with opiate properties

Effects and Precautions:

The medical usage of these drugs (especially in the case of codeine) is for pain relief. It does wonders as a cough suppressant. These drugs are also used to medically treat the withdrawal effects of one another. The main reason for the abuse of these drugs is the temporary state of Euphoria that is produced. The negative side effects include constipation, constriction of the pupils, drowsiness, respiratory depression, itching, nausea and vomiting.

An overdose of narcotics can be fatal! Most narcotic fatalities involve heroin and there are a number of reasons why. The first is that the drug effects brain function, causing the abuser to stop breathing, their blood pressure to fall and their lungs to fill with fluid. Another reason for the death rate of heroin is that many people are allergic to the drug.

The non-fatal symptoms of a narcotics overdose include drowsiness, itchy skin, sweating, vomiting, dilated pupils, a slow pulse and breathing, fluid in the lungs and seizures. Narcotics can often be detected several days after the last usage, through a standard urine test.

In response to an overdose, the first step is to keep the person breathing. This can be done by applying painful stimulus to the body. This must be done carefully, but it is the antidote to narcotics. The next step is to get your patient to a physician who will administer a narcotic antagonist. These can neutralize the effects of narcotics. The response is rapid, with the person acting "normal" within seconds. Street remedies are not recommended, but they include injections of salt or vinegar. As stated previously, pain is "the" antidote to the effects of narcotics.

In all cases, withdrawal from narcotics causes the patient to experience great anxiety and panicky behavior. It is common for a recovering narcotic to seek more of their drug while going through withdrawal. Withdrawal from narcotics is an extremely painful experience which causes the patient to feel as though they are dying, although there is **no** danger of death in uncomplicated cases. The stages of withdrawal are as follows:

Mild – craving for drugs, yawning, tearing eyes, runny nose, insomnia.

Moderate – "Goose bumps," sweating, dilated pupils, muscle spasms, muscle cramps and aching, loss of appetite.

Severe – vomiting, diarrhea, increased blood pressure, temperature and respiration, heightened white blood cell count, orgasm without sexual contact.

In all cases, medical care is required. As the patient will likely search out more of their drug, they should be kept in a "guarded" location, such as a hospital until they feel more like their normal self. It may take up to a few years for their sleep routine to return to normal.

Narcotic Antagonists

Classification:	Narcotic antagonists
Type:	Legal By Prescription and Illegal
Common chemical substances:	These drugs are derived from narcotics
Methods of abuse:	These drugs are usually swallowed

Commonly available forms:	Name	Chemical
	Talwin	Pentazocine
	Narcan	Nalozone
	Nalline	Nalorphan
	Lorfan	Levalorphan
	Cyclazocine	
	Naltrexone	

Effects and Precautions:

Of the drugs in this group, Talwin is the one that most problematic. It is the only drug used for pain relief, and it is also the only drug actually abused. Many physicians abuse this drug. The effects of the other drugs in this group include dysphoria and a blockage of the affects of narcotics. Some users of this drug have reported hallucinations, especially with Nalline and Cyclazocine.

Physical dependence can emerge after prolonged usage. However, the symptoms of withdrawal are mild, usually requiring no medical treatment. One of the withdrawal experiences that makes this drug group stand out among the others is the sensation of "electrical shocks." These are generally startling, but tend to be brief.

The main purpose of all narcotic antagonists is to reverse the effects of narcotics after an overdose. The drug of choice for this is naloxone because of its lack of side effects. These drugs also have the experimental use of preventing narcotic relapse. The reasoning is that if a user takes the narcotic antagonist, and then takes a narcotic, there will be no sense of euphoria.

Neuroleptics (Major Tranquilizers)

Classification: Psycho-Active, anti-psychotic
Type: Legal By Prescription
Common chemical substances: Phenothiazines, Butyrophenones, and Thixoanthenes
Methods of abuse: Most commonly, these are taken orally, but they can be injected.

Commonly available forms:	Name	Chemical
	Thorazine	Chlorpromazine
	Mellaril	Thioridazine
	Stelazine	Trifluperazine
	Compazine	Prochlorperazine
	Trilafon	Perphenazine
	Proxilin	Fluphenazine
	Haldol	Haloperidol
	Navane	Thiothizene
	Taracten	Chlorprothixene
	Serpasil	Reserpine
	Moban	Molindone
	Loxitane	Methapyrilene

Effects and Precautions:

The use of these drugs are for the purpose of calming severe anxiety produced by fear and panic. These drugs also control disturbed behavior as well as hallucinations. When these drugs were discovered in the 1950's, many mental patients were released from hospitals, through the usage of these "wonder" drugs.

Side effects may include Parkinson-like symptoms including tremors, rigidity and a shuffling gait. The most common complaint is dry mouth. These drugs have also been shown to have a destructive influence on the brain, therefore patients who are not psychotic should never take these for periods longer than 3 months.

These drugs are rarely overdosed on, or taken for "a high" because they rank among the more unpleasant drugs. However, these drugs have been used in suicide attempts. As with all cases of overdose, medical help should be obtained.

Stimulants

Classification:	Stimulants
Type:	Legal By Prescription and Illegal
Common chemical substances:	Amphetamines, Cocaine, others
Methods of abuse:	Oral Ingestion, Inhaling, or Intravenous

Commonly available forms:	Name	Chemical
	Benzedrine	Amphetamine
	Dexedrine	Dextro-amphetamine
	Methedrine	Methamphetamine
	Biphetamine	
	Cocaine	Benzymethylecgonine
	Ritalin	Methylphenidate
	Preludin	Phenmetrazine
	Tenuate	Diethylpropion
	INH	Isoniazid
	Coffee, colas, tea, etc.	Caffeine
	Tobacco	Nicotine

Effects and Precautions:

There are four basic reasons that individuals choose to use and abuse these drugs. The number one reason is to "get high." It is a recreational habit. Then there is the sense of status and prestige, which comes especially through the abuse of cocaine. These drugs are also used as a means of staying awake and alert. Many times, these drugs are used to suppress the appetite and control weight.

There are also four methods of use/abuse. Oral amphetamines are the frequent method of prescription users. Then there is snorting, which applies to the recreational user. Intravenous use of amphetamines is perhaps the most addictive as well as the most dangerous. It leads to a massive depression following its "super high." Inhalation is also a "high dose" method, similar to Intravenous use. It is also highly dangerous.

Intoxication by these drugs varies from person to person and from drug to drug. As time goes by, and the body builds up defenses to a drug, more quantities of it are required to reach the previous "high." The effect of these drugs is a stimulation of the central nervous system, which brings with it, an increase in awareness, motor and mental activity as well as suppression of appetite and the need for sleep.

These drugs can, in any amount, cause permanent brain damage to abusers. Intravenous use, specifically, has been connected to a decreased ability to learn. Toxic psychosis can occur in response to any amount of these drugs. This leads to paranoia, and suspicion. These symptoms can generally be treated with major tranquilizers, but hospitalization is usually required.

In response to an overdose, the first step is to provide standard first-aid. You must treat for shock, respiratory or cardiac collapse. You must also provide a calm, quiet place where the person is protected from harming himself/herself, and others. You must give interpersonal support, and never leave them alone. Be very conscientious about personal space. A user who is "strung out" will not permit you to touch him/her.

While going through withdrawal, some common signs are fatigue, extreme hunger or no desire for food, long lasting insomnia, an increase in REM sleep and depression to the point of suicide. In some very rare cases, hallucinations might occur. While going through withdrawal from caffeine (coffee, tea and most soda soft drinks) headaches are very common.

Club Drugs

"Club drugs" are often used by young adults at all-night dance parties, such as "raves" or "trances," dance clubs, and bars. But in the past few years, these drugs have been found increasingly in more mainstream settings.

"Club drug" is a vague term that refers to a wide variety of drugs including MDMA (Ecstasy), GHB, Rohypnol, ketamine, methamphetamine, and LSD. Uncertainties about the drug sources, pharmacological agents, chemicals used to manufacture them, and possible contaminates make it difficult to determine toxicity, consequences, and symptoms.

Classification:	Stimulant amphetamine and hallucinogen mescaline.
Type:	Methylenedioxymethamphetamine (MDMA)
Street Slang:	Ecstasy, XTC, X, Adam, Clarity, Lover's Speed

Methods of abuse:	These are taken orally.

Classification:	
Type:	Gamma-hydroxybutyrate (GHB)
Street Slang:	Grievous Bodily Harm, G, Liquid Ecstacy, Georgia Home, Boy
Methods of abuse:	It is taken orally.

Classification:	Anesthetic
Type:	Ketamine
Street Slang:	Special K, K, Vitamin K, Cat Valiums
Methods of abuse:	Injected, snorted, or smoked

Classification:	Benzodiazepines
Type:	Rohypnol
Street Slang:	Roofies, Rophies, Roche, Forget-me Pill
Common chemical substances:	Flunitrazepam
Methods of abuse:	Usually it is taken orally.

Classification:	Stimulant
Type:	Methamphetamine
Street Slang:	Speed, Ice, Chalk, Meth, Crystal, Crank, Fire, Glass
Methods of abuse:	Smoked, snorted, injected, or ingested orally.

Classification:	Hallucinogen
Type:	Lysergic Acid Diethylamide (LSD)
Street Slang:	Acid, Boomers, Yellow Sunshines
Methods of abuse:	Taken orally in tablet, capsule or liquid forms or on pieces of blotter paper that have absorbed the drug.

Prescription Drugs

Most people who take prescription medications take them responsibly; however, the nonmedical use or abuse of prescription drugs remains a serious public health concern. Certain prescription drugs – opioids, central nervous system (CNS) depressants, and stimulants – when abused, can alter the brain's activity and lead to dependence and possibly addiction.

An estimated 9 million people aged 12 and older used prescription drugs for nonmedical reasons in 1999; more than a quarter of that number reported using prescription drugs nonmedically for the first time in the previous year.

According to a recent national survey of primary care physicians find it difficult to discuss prescription drug abuse with their patients.

Prescription drug abuse is not a new problem, but one that deserves renewed attention. We hope this scientific report is useful to the public, particularly to individuals working with the elderly, who because of the number of medications they may take for various medical conditions, may be more vulnerable to misuse or abuse of prescribed medications. – taken from Research Reports by Alan I. Leshner, Ph.D.

Trends in Prescription Drug Abuse

Several indicators suggest that prescription drug abuse is on the rise in the United States. According to the 1999 National Household Survey on Drug Abuse, in 1998, an estimated 1.6 million Americans used prescription pain relievers nonmedically for the first time. This represents a significant increase since the 1980s, when there were generally fewer than 500,000 first-time users per year. From 1990 to 1998, the number of new users of pain relievers increased by 181 percent; the number of individuals who initiated tranquilizer use increased by 132 percent; the number of new sedative users increased by 90 percent; and the number of people initiating stimulant use increased by 165 percent. In 1999, an estimated 4 million people - almost 2 percent of the population aged 12 and older - were currently (use in past month) using certain prescription drugs nonmedically: pain relievers (2.6 million users), sedatives and tranquilizers (1.3 million users), and stimulants (0.9 million users).

Although prescription drug abuse affects many Americans, some trends of concern can be seen among older adults, adolescents, and women. In addition, health care professionals - including physicians, nurses, pharmacists, dentists, anesthesiologists, and veterinarians - may be at increased risk of prescription drug abuse because of ease of access, as well as their ability to self-prescribe drugs. In spite of this increased risk, recent surveys and research in the early 1990s indicate that health care providers probably suffer from substance abuse, including alcohol and drugs, at a rate similar to rates in society as a whole, in the range of 8 to 12 percent.

Older adults

The misuse of prescription drugs may be the most common form of drug abuse among the elderly. Elderly persons use prescription medications approximately three times as frequently as the general population and have been found to have the poorest rates of compliance with directions for taking a medication. In addition, data from the Veterans Affairs Hospital System suggest that elderly patients may be prescribed inappropriately high doses of medications such as benzodiazepines and may be prescribed these medications for longer periods than are younger adults. In general, older people should be prescribed lower doses of medications, because the body's ability to metabolize many medications decreases with age.

An association between age-related morbidity and abuse of prescription medications likely exists. For example, elderly persons who take benzodiazepines are at increased risk for falls that cause hip and thigh fractures, as well as for vehicle accidents. Cognitive impairment also is associated with benzodiazepine use, although memory impairment may be reversible when the drug is discontinued. Finally, use of benzodiazepines for longer than 4 months is not recommended for elderly patients because of the possibility of physical dependence.

Adolescents and young adults

Data from the National Household Survey on Drug Abuse indicate that the most dramatic increase in new users of prescription drugs for nonmedical purposes occurs in 12- to 17-year-olds and 18- to 25-year-olds. In addition, 12- to 14-year-olds reported psychotherapeutics (for example, painkillers or stimulants) as one of two primary drugs used. The 1999 Monitoring the Future survey showed that for barbiturates, tranquilizers, and narcotics other than heroin, the general, long-term declines in use among young adults in the 1980s leveled off in the early 1990s, with modest increases again in the mid- to late 1990s. For example, the use of methylphenidate (Ritalin) among high school seniors increased from an annual prevalence (use of the drug within the preceding year) of 0.1

percent in 1992 to an annual prevalence of 2.8 percent in 1997 before reaching a plateau.

It also appears that college students' nonmedical use of pain relievers such as oxycodone with aspirin (Percodan) and hydrocodone (Vicodin) is on the rise. The 1999 Drug Abuse Warning Network, which collects data on drug-related episodes in hospital emergency departments, reported that mentions of hydrocodone as a cause for visiting an emergency room increased by 37 percent among all age groups from 1997 to 1999. Mentions of the benzodiazepine clonazepam (Klonopin) increased by 102 percent since 1992.

Gender differences

Studies suggest that women are more likely than men to be prescribed an abusable prescription drug, particularly narcotics and anti-anxiety drugs - in some cases 48 percent more likely.

Overall, men and women have roughly similar rates of nonmedical use of prescription drugs. An exception is found among 12- to 17-year-olds: In this age group, young women are more likely than young men to use psychotherapeutic drugs nonmedically.

In addition, research has shown that women and men who use prescription opioids are equally likely to become addicted. However, among women and men who use either a sedative, anti-anxiety drug, or hypnotic, women are almost two times more likely to become addicted.

What are some of the commonly abused prescription drugs?

Although many prescription drugs can be abused or misused, there are three classes of prescription drugs that are most commonly abused:

- Opioids, which are most often prescribed to treat pain;

- CNS depressants, which are used to treat anxiety and sleep disorders;

- Stimulants, which are prescribed to treat the sleep disorder narcolepsy, attention-deficit hyperactivity disorder (ADHD), and obesity.

Opioids

What are opioids?

Opioids are commonly prescribed because of their effective analgesic, or pain-relieving, properties. Medications that fall within this class - sometimes referred to as narcotics - include morphine, codeine, and related drugs. Morphine, for example, is often used before or after surgery to alleviate severe pain. Codeine, because it is less efficacious than morphine, is used for milder pain. Other examples of opioids that can be prescribed to alleviate pain include oxycodone (OxyContin), propoxyphene (Darvon), hydrocodone (Vicodin), and hydromorphone (Dilaudid), as well as meperidine (Demerol), which is used less often because of its side effects. In addition to their pain-relieving properties, some of these drugs - for example, codeine and diphenoxylate (Lomotil) - can be used to relieve coughs and diarrhea.

How do opioids affect the brain and body?

Opioids act by attaching to specific proteins called opioid receptors, which are found in the brain, spinal cord, and gastrointestinal tract. When these drugs attach to certain opioid receptors, they can block the transmission of pain messages to the brain. In addition, opioids can produce drowsiness, cause constipation, and, depending upon the amount of drug taken, depress respiration. Opioid drugs also can cause euphoria by affecting the brain regions that mediate what we perceive as pleasure.

What are the possible consequences of opioid use and abuse?

Chronic use of opioids can result in tolerance for the drugs, which means that users must take higher doses to achieve the same initial effects. Long-term use also can lead to physical dependence and addiction - the body adapts to the presence of the drug, and withdrawal symptoms occur if use is reduced or stopped. Symptoms of withdrawal include restlessness, muscle and bone pain, insomnia, diarrhea, vomiting, cold flashes with goose bumps ("cold turkey"), and involuntary leg movements. Finally, taking a large single dose of an opioid could cause severe respiratory depression that can lead to death. Many studies have shown, however, that properly managed medical use of opioid analgesic drugs is safe and rarely causes clinical addiction, defined as compulsive, often uncontrollable use of drugs. Taken exactly as prescribed, opioids can be used to manage pain effectively.

Is it safe to use opioid drugs with other medications?

Opioids are safe to use with other drugs only under a physician's supervision. Typically, they should not be used with other substances that depress the central nervous system, such as alcohol, antihistamines, barbiturates, benzodiazepines, or general anesthetics, as such a combination increases the risk of life-threatening respiratory depression.

CNS depressants

What are CNS depressants?

CNS depressants are substances that can slow normal brain function. Because of this property, some CNS depressants are useful in the treatment of anxiety and sleep disorders. Among the medications that are commonly prescribed for these purposes are the following:

- Barbiturates, such as mephobarbital (Mebaral) and pentobarbital sodium (Nembutal), which are used to treat anxiety, tension, and sleep disorders.

- Benzodiazepines, such as diazepam (Valium), chlordiazepoxide HCl (Librium), and alprazolam (Xanax), which can be prescribed to treat anxiety, acute stress reactions, and panic attacks; the more sedating benzodiazepines, such as triazolam (Halcion) and estazolam (ProSom) can be prescribed for short-term treatment of sleep disorders.

In higher doses, some CNS depressants can be used as general anesthetics.

How do CNS depressants affect the brain and body?

There are numerous CNS depressants; most act on the brain by affecting the neurotransmitter gamma-aminobutyric acid (GABA). Neurotransmitters are brain chemicals that facilitate communication between brain cells. GABA works by decreasing brain activity. Although the different classes of CNS depressants work in unique ways, ultimately

118

it is through their ability to increase GABA activity that they produce a drowsy or calming effect that is beneficial to those suffering from anxiety or sleep disorders.

What are the possible consequences of CNS depressant use and abuse?

Despite their many beneficial effects, barbiturates and benzodiazepines have the potential for abuse and should be used only as prescribed. During the first few days of taking a prescribed CNS depressant, a person usually feels sleepy and uncoordinated, but as the body becomes accustomed to the effects of the drug, these feelings begin to disappear. If one uses these drugs long term, the body will develop tolerance for the drugs, and larger doses will be needed to achieve the same initial effects. In addition, continued use can lead to physical dependence and - when use is reduced or stopped - withdrawal. Because all CNS depressants work by slowing the brain's activity, when an individual stops taking them, the brain's activity can rebound and race out of control, possibly leading to seizures and other harmful consequences. Although withdrawal from benzodiazepines can be problematic, it is rarely life threatening, whereas withdrawal from prolonged use of other CNS depressants can have life-threatening complications. Therefore, someone who is thinking about discontinuing CNS depressant therapy or who is suffering withdrawal from a CNS depressant should speak with a physician or seek medical treatment.

Is it safe to use CNS depressants with other medications?

CNS depressants should be used with other medications only under a physician's supervision. Typically, they should not be combined with any other medication or substance that causes CNS depression, including prescription pain medicines, some over-the-counter cold and allergy medications, or alcohol. Using CNS depressants with these other substances - particularly alcohol - can slow breathing, or slow both the heart and respiration, and possibly lead to death.

Stimulants

What are stimulants?

As the name suggests, stimulants are a class of drugs that enhance brain activity - they cause an increase in alertness, attention, and energy that is accompanied by elevated blood pressure and increased heart rate and respiration. Stimulants were used historically to treat asthma and other respiratory problems, obesity, neurological disorders, and a variety of other ailments. But as their potential for abuse and addiction became apparent, the medical use of stimulants began to wane. Now, stimulants are prescribed for the treatment of only a few health conditions, including narcolepsy, attention-deficit hyperactivity disorder, and depression that has not responded to other treatments. Stimulants may be used as appetite suppressants for short-term treatment of obesity, and they also may be used for patients with asthma.

How do stimulants affect the brain and body?

Stimulants, such as dextroamphetamine (Dexedrine) and methylphenidate (Ritalin), have chemical structures that are similar to a family of key brain neurotransmitters called monoamines, which include norepinephrine and dopamine. Stimulants increase the amount of these chemicals in the brain. This, in turn, increases blood pressure and heart rate, constricts blood vessels, increases blood glucose, and opens up the pathways of the respiratory system. In addition, the increase in dopamine is associated with a sense of euphoria that can accompany the use of these drugs.

What are the possible consequences of stimulant use and abuse?

The consequences of stimulant abuse can be dangerous. Although their use may not lead to physical dependence and risk of withdrawal, stimulants can be addictive in that individuals begin to use them compulsively. Taking high doses of some stimulants repeatedly over a short time can lead to feelings of hostility or paranoia. Additionally, taking high doses of a stimulant may result in dangerously high body temperatures and an irregular heartbeat. There is also the potential for cardiovascular failure or lethal seizures.

Is it safe to use stimulants with other medications?

Stimulants should be used with other medications only when the patient is under a physician's supervision. For example, a stimulant may be prescribed to a patient taking an antidepressant. However, health care providers and patients should be mindful that antidepressants enhance the effects of a stimulant. Patients also should be aware that stimulants should not be mixed with over-the-counter cold medicines that contain decongestants, as this combination may cause blood pressure to become dangerously high or lead to irregular heart rhythms.

Some Commonly Prescribed Medications: Use and Consequences		
Opioids	**CNS Depressants**	**Stimulants**

• Oxycodone (OxyContin)
 	
• Propoxyphen (Darvon)
 	
• Hydrocodone (Vicodin)
 	
• Hydromorphone (Dilaudid)
 	
• Meperidine (Demerol)
 	
• Diphenoxylate (Lomotil)
	Barbiturates
	
	  • Mephobarbital (Mebaral)
	
	  • Pentobarbital sodium (Nembutal)
	
	Benzodiazepines
	
	  • Diazepam (Valium)
	
	  • Chlordiazepoxide hydrochloride (Librium)
	
	  • Alprazolam (Xanax)
	
	  • Triazolam (Halcion)
	
	  • Estazolam (ProSom)
		• Dextroamphetamine (Dexedrine)
		
		• Methylphenidate (Ritalin)
		
		• Sibutramine hydrochloride monohydrate (Meridia)

Generally prescribed for	Generally prescribed for	Generally prescribed for
• Postsurgical pain relief • Management of acute or chronic pain • Relief of coughs and diarrhea	• Anxiety • Tensions • Panic attacks • Acute stress reactions • Sleep disorders • Anesthesia (at high does)	• Narcolepsy • Attention-deficit hyperactivity disorder (ADHD) • Depression that does not respond to other treatment • Short-term treatment of obesity • Asthma
In the body Opioids attach to opioid receptors in the brain and spinal cord, blocking the transmission of pain messages to the brain.	**In the body** CNS depressants slow brain activity through actions on the GABA system and, therefore, produce a calming effect.	**In the body** Stimulants enhance brain activity, causing an increase in alertness, attention, and energy.
Effects of short-term use • Blocked pain messages • Drowsiness • Constipation • Depressed respiration (depending on dose)	**Effects of short-term use** • A "sleepy" and uncoordinated feeling during the first few days, as the body becomes accustomed – tolerant – to the effects, these feelings	**Effects of short-term use** • Elevated blood pressure • Increased heart rate • Increased respiration • Suppressed appetite

	diminish.	• Sleep deprivation
Effects of long-term use	**Effects of long-term use**	**Effects of long-term use**
• Potential for tolerance, physical dependence, withdrawal, and/or addiction	• Potential for tolerance, physical dependence, withdrawal, and/or addiction	• Potential for addiction
Possible negative effects	**Possible negative effects**	**Possible negative effects**
• Severe respiratory depression or death following a large single dose	• Seizures following a rebound in brain activity after reducing or discontinuing use	• Dangerously high body temperatures or an irregular heartbeat after taking high doses • Cardiovascular failure or lethal seizures • For some stimulants, hostility or feelings of paranoia after taking high does repeatedly over a short period of time
Should not be used with Other substances that cause CNS depression, including	**Should not be used with** Other substances that cause CNS depression, including	**Should not be used with** • Over-the-counter could medicines containing decongestants • Antidepressants,

• Alcohol	• Alcohol	unless supervise by a physicians
• Antihistamines	• Prescription opioid pain medicines	• Some asthma medications
• Barbiturates		
• Benzodiazepines	• Some over-the-counter cold and allergy medications	
• General anesthetics		

What are anabolic steroids?

"Anabolic steroids" is the familiar name for synthetic substances related to the male sex hormones (androgens). They promote the growth of skeletal muscle (anabolic effects) and the development of male sexual characteristics (androgenic effects), and also have some other effects. The term "anabolic steroids" will be used through-out this report because of its familiarity, although the proper term for these compounds is "anabolic-androgenic" steroids.

Anabolic steroids were developed in the late 1930s primarily to treat hypogonadism, a condition in which the testes do not produce sufficient testosterone for normal growth, development, and sexual functioning. The primary medical uses of these compounds are to treat delayed puberty, some types of impotence, and wasting of the body caused by HIV infection or other diseases.

During the 1930s, scientists discovered that anabolic steroids could facilitate the growth of skeletal muscle in laboratory animals, which led to use of the compounds first by bodybuilders and weightlifters and then by athletes in other sports. Steroid abuse has become so widespread in athletics that it affects the outcome of sports contests.

More than 100 different anabolic steroids have been developed, but they require a prescription to be used legally in the United States. Most steroids that are used illegally are smuggled in from other countries, illegally diverted from U.S. pharmacies, or synthesized in clandestine laboratories.

What are steroidal supplements?

In the United States, supplements such as dehydroepian-drosterone (DHEA) and androstenedione (street name Andro) can be purchased legally without a prescription through many commercial sources including health food stores. They are often referred to as dietary supplements, although they are not food products. They are often taken because the user believes they have anabolic effects.

Steroidal supplements can be converted into testosterone (an important male sex hormone) or a similar compound in the body. Whether such conversion produces sufficient quantities of testosterone to promote muscle growth or whether the supplements themselves promote muscle growth is unknown. Little is known about the side effects of steroidal supplements, but if large quantities of these compounds substantially increase testosterone levels in the body, they also are likely to produce the same side effects as anabolic steroids.

What is the scope of steroid abuse in the United States?

Recent evidence suggests that steroid abuse among adolescents is on the rise. The 1999 Monitoring the Future study, a NIDA-funded survey of drug abuse among adolescents in middle and high schools across the United States, estimated that 2.7 percent of 8th- and 10th-graders and 2.9 percent of 12th-graders had taken anabolic steroids at least once in their lives. For 10th-graders, that is a significant increase from 1998, when 2.0 percent of 10th-graders said they had taken anabolic steroids at least once. For all three grades, the 1999 levels represent a significant increase from 1991, the first year that data on steroid abuse were collected from the younger students. In that year, 1.9 percent of 8th-graders, 1.8 percent of 10th-graders, and 2.1 percent of 12th-graders reported that they had taken anabolic steroids at least once.

Few data exist on the extent of steroid abuse by adults. It has been estimated that hundreds of thousands of people aged 18 and older abuse anabolic steroids at least once a year.

Among both adolescents and adults, steroid abuse is higher among males than females. However, steroid abuse is growing most rapidly among young women.

Why do people abuse anabolic steroids?

One of the main reasons people give for abusing steroids is to improve their performance in sports. Among competitive bodybuilders, steroid abuse has been estimated to be very high. Among other athletes, the incidence of abuse probably varies depending on the specific sport.

Another reason people give for taking steroids is to increase their muscle size and/or reduce their body fat. This group includes some people who have a behavioral syndrome (muscle dysmorphia) in which a person has a distorted image of his or her body. Men with this condition think that they look small and weak, even if they are large and muscular. Similarly, women with the syndrome think that they look fat and flabby, even though they are actually lean and muscular.

Some people who abuse steroids to boost muscle size have experienced physical or sexual abuse. They are trying to increase their muscle size to protect themselves. In one series of interviews with male weightlifters, 25 percent who abused steroids reported memories of childhood physical or sexual abuse, compared with none who did not abuse steroids. In a study of women weightlifters, twice as many of those who had been raped reported using anabolic steroids and/or another purported muscle-building drug, compared to those who had not been raped. Moreover, almost all of those who had been raped reported that they markedly increased their bodybuilding activities after the attack. They believed that being bigger and stronger would discourage further attacks because men would find them either intimidating or unattractive.

Finally, some adolescents abuse steroids as part of a pattern of high-risk behaviors. These adolescents also take risks such as drinking and driving, carrying a gun, not wearing a helmet on a motorcycle, and abusing other illicit drugs.

While conditions such as muscle dysmorphia, a history of physical or sexual abuse, or a history of engaging in high-risk behaviors may increase the risk of initiating or continuing steroid abuse, researchers agree that most steroid abusers are psychologically normal when they start abusing the drugs.

How are anabolic steroids used?

Some anabolic steroids are taken orally, others are injected intramuscularly, and still others are provided in gels or creams that are rubbed on the skin. Doses taken by abusers can be 10 to 100 times higher than the doses used for medical conditions.

Steroid abusers typically "stack" the drugs, meaning that they take two or more different anabolic steroids, mixing oral and/or injectable types and sometimes even including compounds that are designed for veterinary use. Abusers think that the different steroids interact to produce an effect on muscle size that is greater than the effects of each drug individually, a theory that has not been tested scientifically.

Often, steroid abusers also "pyramid" their doses in cycles of 6 to 12 weeks. At the beginning of a cycle, the person starts with low doses of the drugs being stacked and then slowly increases the doses. In the second half of the cycle, the doses are slowly decreased to zero. This is sometimes followed by a second cycle in which the person continues to train but without drugs. Abusers believe that pyramiding allows the body time to adjust to the high doses and the drug-free cycle allows the body's hormonal system time to recuperate. As with stacking, the perceived benefits of pyramiding and cycling have not been substantiated scientifically.

What are the health consequences of steroid abuse?

Anabolic steroid abuse has been associated with a wide range of adverse side effects ranging from some that are physically unattractive, such as acne and breast development in men, to others that are life threatening, such as heart attacks and liver cancer. Most are reversible if the abuser stops taking the drugs, but some are permanent.

Most data on the long-term effects of anabolic steroids on humans come from case reports rather than formal epidemiological studies. From the case reports, the incidence of life-threatening effects appears to be low, but serious adverse effects may be under-recognized or under-reported. Data from animal studies seem to support this possibility. One study found that exposing male mice for one-fifth of their lifespan to steroid doses comparable to those taken by human athletes caused a high percentage of premature deaths.

Hormonal system

Steroid abuse disrupts the normal production of hormones in the body, causing both reversible and irreversible changes. Changes that can be reversed include reduced sperm production and shrinking of the testicles (testicular atrophy). Irreversible changes include male-pattern baldness and breast development (gynecomastia). In one study of male bodybuilders, more than half had testicular atrophy, and more than half had gynecomastia. Gynecomastia is thought to occur due to the disruption of normal hormone balance. In the female body, anabolic steroids cause masculinization. Breast size and body fat decrease, the skin becomes coarse, the clitoris enlarges, and the voice deepens. Women may experience excessive growth of body hair but lose scalp hair. With continued administration of steroids, some of these effects are irreversible.

Musculoskeletal system

Rising levels of testosterone and other sex hormones normally trigger the growth spurt that occurs during puberty and adolescence. Subsequently, when these hormones reach certain levels, they signal the bones to stop growing, locking a person into his or her maximum height.

When a child or adolescent takes anabolic steroids, the resulting artificially high sex hormone levels can signal the bones to stop growing sooner than they normally would have done.

Cardiovascular system

Steroid abuse has been associated with cardiovascular diseases (CVD), including heart attacks and strokes, even in athletes younger than 30. Steroids contribute to the development of CVD, partly by changing the levels of lipoproteins that carry cholesterol in the blood. Steroids, particularly the oral types, increase the level of low-density lipoprotein (LDL) and decrease the level of high-density lipoprotein (HDL). High LDL and low HDL levels increase the risk of atherosclerosis, a condition in which fatty substances are deposited inside arteries and disrupt blood flow. If blood is prevented from reaching the heart, the result can be a heart attack. If blood is prevented from reaching the brain, the result can be a stroke.

Steroids also increase the risk that blood clots will form in blood vessels, potentially disrupting blood flow and damaging the heart muscle so that it does not pump blood effectively.

Liver

Steroid abuse has been associated with liver tumors and a rare condition called peliosis hepatis, in which blood-filled cysts form in the liver. Both the tumors and the cysts sometimes rupture, causing internal bleeding.

Skin

Steroid abuse can cause acne, cysts, and oily hair and skin.

Infection

Many abusers who inject anabolic steroids use nonsterile injection techniques or share contaminated needles with other abusers. In addition, some steroid preparations are manufactured illegally under non-sterile conditions. These factors put abusers at risk for acquiring life-threatening viral infections, such as HIV and hepatitis B and C. Abusers also can develop infective endocarditis, a bacterial illness that causes a potentially fatal inflammation of the inner lining of the heart. Bacterial infections also can cause pain and abscess formation at injection sites.

Chapter Nine Questions

1. Describe the effects of alcohol.

2. Describe the effects of antidepressants.

3. Describe the effects of barbiturates.

4. Describe the effects of hallucinogens.

5. Describe the effects of marijuana.

6. Describe the effects of minor tranquilizers.

7. Describe the effects of narcotics and opiates.

8. Describe the effects of narcotic antagonists.

9. Describe the effects of neuroleptics.

10. Describe the effects of stimulants.

11. Describe the effects of club drugs.

12. Describe the effects of abused prescription medication.

Chapter Ten

The Process Of Physical Addiction

The Brain is a very complex and functional unit. It is made up of billions of tiny nerve cells known as neurons which communicate with one another through the use of chemical signals. At its core, the brain works on a system of reward. An example might be that you eat a piece of chocolate, it tastes good, it feels good in your mouth, and then you swallow. This idea of, or sensation that it is "good" is the reward. The next time you are offered a piece of chocolate, you will probably accept.

How Information Travels Through The Brain

The brain can be divided into many different regions, based on function. For instance, there are regions which control movement, memory, reward, vision, judgment, sensation and coordination. The reward center of the brain has the sole purpose of reinforcing certain behaviors. As an individual takes drugs, neurons travel down the reward pathway, which extends from the ventral tegmental area (VTA) to the nucleas accumbens and on to the prefrontal cortex, thus activating the pathway and reinforcing their destructive behaviors.

The pathways in the brain are made up of neurons. These neurons are real, and can actually be seen under a powerful microscope. The neuron is comprised of four main parts, the soma, dendrite, axon and the terminal. In a normal case, information travels from neuron to neuron, the soma and dendrites receive chemical information from their neighboring neuronal axons. This chemical information is then converted to electrical pulses, which meet on the soma. This creates a large impulse, often called action potential, which travels down the axon toward the terminal.

Vesicles which contain neurotransmitters such as dopamine will move toward the presynaptic membrane as an electrical impulse arrives at the neuron's terminal. Once inside the synaptic cleft, the dopamine can bind itself to special proteins, called dopamine receptors, which are attached to the membranes of neighboring neurons. When the receptors are occupied to neurotransmitters, various cellular actions take place: enzymes can be activated or inhibited, certain ions may be given permission to enter or exit.

As the dopamine molecule binds to the dopamine receptor, it comes off the receptor and is removed from the synaptic cleft by uptake pumps. This is done so that not too much dopamine is ever present in the synaptic cleft at any one time. Some neighboring neurons release a compound known as a neuromodulator. These "endorphins" bind to opiate receptors which reside on the post-synaptic cell. In some cases they land on the terminals of other neurons. Instead of being removed by the uptake pumps, as is the case with dopamine, neuromodulators such as endorphins are destroyed by enzymes.

Once the dopamine is bound to the receptor, and before it is removed by the uptake pump, another protein, the G-protein, comes close to the receptor and begins transmitting signals to the enzymes telling them to produce cyclic adenosine monophosphate, also known as cAMP, within the cell that the receptor is attached to. In some cases, this transmission can signal a decrease in cAMP production as well. This depends on the type of dopamine receptor and G-protein present. The chemical cAMP controls a cell's ability to generate electrical impulses as well as other vital cellular functions.

This is how information travels from neuron to neuron in the brain! These chemical changes happen rapidly and constantly, with each thought. As information travels to a neuron's terminal, neurotransmitters (dopamine), are released and these bind themselves to the receptors of neighboring neurons. From neuron to neuron.

Rewards

As stated earlier, positive reinforcement, or reward, play a vital role in the choices we make. Will we choose to have another piece of chocolate? Much study has been conducted with laboratory rats as it relates to the concept of reward. In the lab, rats will press a bar to get an injection of cocaine or heroin. The rat will continue pressing the bar because of the "reward" that it brings.

In life, there are natural reward. These are water, food and sex. Without these, the survival of any species is doomed. Both animals and people will continue behavior so long as it is rewarding – take work for instance. They will then cease these behaviors once they are no longer rewarding – would you continue writing service reports for your boss if he fired you? There is actually a part of the brain specifically designated to become active in response to natural and artificial rewards (artificial would include addictive drugs).

As stated earlier, scientists have discovered, with the aid of laboratory rats, that the reward pathway starts with the VTA, moves onto the nucleus accumbens and runs up to the prefrontal cortex. However, not only do scientists know where the reward pathway lies, they know how the drugs interact with it.

How It Works

When a person abuses cocaine, it travels to the brain, quickly reaching all of its various areas. However, it concentrates in certain areas such as the VTA, the nucleus accumbens and the caudate nucleus. Cocaine concentrates itself especially in those areas associated with the reward pathway. Accumulation in the caudate nucleus has been connected to behavioral effects such as pacing, nail-biting, scratching and other "bad habit" behaviors.

When cocaine reaches the brain, it concentrates itself in areas that have a wealth of dopamine synapses. When cocaine is present in the synapse, it will bind itself to the uptake pumps and prevent them from removing dopamine from the synapse. With no way to escape, dopamine continues to accumulate and more dopamine receptors are activated. As dopamine receptors are activated, cAMP is produced. So, in response to the increased receptor activity, cAMP production in the post-synaptic cell is increased. This leads to abnormal "firing" patterns for the cell.

Because of this increased activity in the nucleus accumbens, increased impulses leave the nucleus, activating the reward system. As prolonged cocaine usage continues, this heightened activity in the reward center comes to require the drug to maintain the sensation of reward. As time goes on, the user will eventually be unable to feel the In addition to affecting the reward centers of the brain, cocaine also affects the energy level of the brain as a unit. Positron Emission Tomography (PET) scans are able to show how glucose, the power source for the brain, is metabolized by the brain. Scans have shown that cocaine users have a diminished capacity to metabolize glucose. This leads to reduced brain activity and a disruption of brain function.

Heroin and Morphine work a bit differently than cocaine. These drugs are opiates. When a person takes these drugs, they too travel to the brain, but they concentrate themselves in different areas. They also concentrate in the VTA and the nucleus accumbens (the reward pathway), but they also congregate in the caudate nucleus and the thalamus. Because they gather in the thalamus, these drugs have great ability to produce analgesia.

Opiates activate the reward system using the nucleus accumbens, but their action is a bit more complicated. Three neurons are required to participate in opiate action: the dopamine terminal, another terminal containing a different neurotransmitter, and the post-synaptic cell which contains dopamine receptors. Opiates make contact with the opiate receptors on a neighboring terminal, and this sends a signal telling the dopamine terminal to release more dopamine. With the production of more dopamine, there is an increase in dopamine receptors. This causes an increased production of cAMP, which alters the normal activity of the neuron.

The result of an opiate, as it is with cocaine, is that the activity in the nucleus accumbens stimulates the reward pathways, thus reinforcing the user's desire for the drug. Again, as with cocaine, continued use of the drug will cause the user to receive no pleasure or reward from natural rewards like food, water and sex. Thus, it becomes impossible for the user to function normally without the drug.

THC, the active ingredient in marijuana, travels quickly to the brain. It settles in the VTA, nucleus accumbens, caudate nucleus, hippocampus and cerebellum. These are the areas of the brain which control movement, sensations, coordination, memory, judgement and reward. THC binds to THC receptors found in high amounts in these areas. THC causes memory loss because of its activity in the hippocampus, the major memory center for the brain. Loss of coordination is due to its activity in the cerebellum.

Of the drug types mentioned, scientists know the least about THC. However, there has been much intense study, and much evidence has been uncovered. As with opiates, it is theorized that THC uses three neurons to bring about intoxication: the dopamine terminal, another terminal containing a different neurotransmitter and the post-synaptic cell which contains dopamine receptors.

THC connects itself to the THC receptors on a neighboring terminal. This causes a signal to be sent triggering the dopamine terminal to release more dopamine. Because more dopamine is being released, dopamine receptors become activated. This brings about an elevation in cAMP production inside the post-synaptic cell, altering the normal activity of the neuron. Scientists still do not fully know how marijuana interacts with the reward system, but it is an area of intense study.

All addictive drugs affect the reward pathways in the nucleus accumbens and the VTA. Each affects the neurons in its own way, but the effects are the same, dependence on a chemical based on a habit of rewarding sensations. Alcohol, nicotine, amphetamines and so on all affect the reward center of the brain.

Of course, when a substance used no longer causes the requisite pleasure, more is required. Once *habituation* occurs, the substance is then needed to feel "normal" moving the person towards serious and life threatening addiction.

Chapter Ten Questions for Discussion

1. Name the key components of the brain affected by drug usage.

2. What is the sole purpose of the reward center of the brain?

3. What is dopamine? Why is this substance important?

4. What does the chemical cAMP control?

5. In addition to affecting the reward center of the brain, cocaine affects what else?

6. Do all addictive drugs affect the reward center? Why?

Chapter Eleven

Drug Abuse Treatment and Theory

The Theory of Addiction as Disease

The main purpose for this outlook on addiction is to move the actions associated with addiction from being seen as sin to treatable a (but not curable) disease. Hence the term "treatment." You cannot treat sin, but you can treat a disease.

Many addicts feel more comfortable with the idea of their addiction being the symptom of a greater disease. They are more willing to seek help with a disease than they are with sin. After all, when you are sick, you go to the doctor and he/she takes care of you. But when you are in sin, condemnation is often all you get. The "Disease Model" is best applied to those individuals who have become so dependent that they have real medical complications.

The Psychoanalytic Approach

Psychoanalysis and dynamic psychotherapy are rarely used for the treatment of addiction. However, it does provide a wealth of information as to the underlying forces that may push an individual towards substance addiction. Through the use of this approach, the counselor can learn the addict's hidden defense mechanisms, denial, rationalization, etc., and the root of these particular defenses. Dynamic psychotherapy is especially effective during the early stages of recovery treatment.

This approach is especially effective in determining how compulsive behaviors, such as drug addiction, maybe symptoms of a bigger (or perhaps smaller) problem. Oftentimes, an abuser of a substance uses drugs to immediately gratify their urge for external stimuli. This causes the *ego* (sense of self) to weaken. Therefore, one of the obvious conclusions drawn by the dynamic approach is that the abuser must learn to delay gratification, learn to organize daily activity and make plans which prioritize life's goals, desires, needs and wants.

Conditioning

The central concept of this theory is that reward is the essential driving force behind all human behavior. This theory describes the self-administration of drugs as goal-oriented conduct. That means that the user knows that by taking the drug they will experience a sense of "euphoria." Based on that "reward" they "decide" to take the drug. Over time, they are conditioned to believe that all they have to do is take the drug and they will receive their reward.

This outlook on drug addiction explains why it is so difficult for many abusers to walk away from their drug, and why many who do walk away, eventually pick up the addiction later. During early recovery stages, the abuser will often feel that they are being deprived of their reward. However, at the same time they know that their old rewards are still available in abundance. Relapse is always a possibility, especially during the first year of recovery.

According to this approach, it is necessary to provide to the client a set of non-chemical rewards to choose from. These can include recreational activities, hobbies and other enjoyable pursuits. This can often be a time when the client will remember dreams and goals from childhood. These goals and activities can be an amazing boost to a recovering addict. They can facilitate faster recovery with less struggle.

Social Learning Theory

Similar to the conditioning theory, this theory suggests that alcoholics (or drug users) use their substance, fully expecting to receive some desired effect from the usage. However, this theory differs in that it suggests the reward is not the driving force, but rather the habit. The user learns over time that when they take the drug, they can escape from their troubles.

Because of its focus on the cognitive functioning of individuals, this approach has been successfully used to identify strategies to prevent relapse. One such strategy is called self-efficacy. This is basically the client's belief that he or she is fully able to do whatever is necessary achieve recovery. Some of these tasks may include abstinence from their drug, attendance of counseling sessions as well as taking their prescribed medications.

Clients who lack self-efficacy are likely to relapse. However, there are techniques for boosting self-efficacy which involve the teaching of new or undeveloped skills. Of particular danger to the client with low self-efficacy is a phenomena known as "abstinence violation effect." This basically means that when recovering users "slip" and have a drink of alcohol, they will often condemn themselves, and as a result of low self-image, will continue to drink or abuse their substance of choice rather than stopping.

It is the counselor's duty to teach the client skills which will prevent them from this destructive pattern, thus building self-efficacy. One such skill is to prepare the client for high-risk situations. The client should also understand what the words lapse and relapse really mean. That way they will not feel like failures when they "slip back" a bit. Another vital skill to teach is the identifying of triggers. These include beer commercials, the smell of cigarette smoke, pharmaceutical commercials and so on. The strengthening of a client's self-efficacy skills is the cornerstone of this approach.

Family System's Theory

FaST (Family System's Theory) suggests that an individual's particular drug addiction is founded in a deeper familial need. By this it is meant that an individual subconsciously "chooses" to be an addict or to be severely dysfunctional in order to keep the family focus on the individual's dysfunction, rather than the family's deep, dark secrets. The role of "dysfunctional target" is assigned on a subconscious level, in the same way that the roles of the "hero," "spy" or "victim."

These roles are designed to keep a dysfunctional family "afloat" and to distract its members from dealing with the core issues of the dysfunction. After all, in the subconscious minds of the family members, some issues are bigger than the family, and could lead to its destruction.

During the process of recovery, this subconscious world of role playing can lead to many disturbances. The family's collective unconscious designed each role with specific parameters that must be met. If one role is changed, the addict is no longer an addict, the whole equilibrium of the family is changed, causing unpredictable, and to the family, possibly dangerous results.

This often leads to sabotage. Other members will make efforts to hinder the recovering addict's progress. This could include things like a sudden heart attack by the father, a younger sibling threatening suicide or a parent suddenly dying, seeking divorce or separation. These behaviors can often be attempts to hold the family together, and can drive a recovering addict back to his drug. It is suggested, by proponents of this theory, that addictive counseling and therapy should always include members of the family. After all, it is the role of the therapist to bring good mental health, and though an absence of drug abuse may certainly help, underlying problems must also be dealt with as well.

Chapter Eleven Questions for Discussion

1. What is meant by addiction as a disease?
2. Who can the dynamic approach be helpful in the treatment of addiction?
3. What is the central concept of the conditioning theory?
4. Explain Social Learning Theory.
5. What is self-efficacy?
6. Why is it important for the client to understand what lapse and relapse truly mean?
7. Describe the Family System Theory. How might this method be helpful in Christian families?

Chapter Twelve

Cognitive Behavior Therapy

The Benefits of Cognitive Behavior Therapy (CBT)

CBT is a short-term approach toward treating addictive behavior. It is especially suited to clinical programs whose time and financial resources are stretched thin. CBT is a highly structured approach which uses goals which focus on the day to day problems that cocaine and other drug abusers face as they struggle to stay free of their drug. The CBT approach is also highly personalized to the individual in need. Its principles can be applied and tailored to just about any individual's personal needs. It can also be adapted to a group therapy format. One of the greatest benefits of CBT is the fact that it teaches skills to the patient which can be used throughout the rest of their life.

CBT can be divided into two primary components: functional analysis and the teaching of skills. During treatment, whenever the client uses drugs, the therapist walks him/her through a process which identifies the client's thoughts, feelings and pre-cursor behavior leading up to the abuse. This gives the client a roadmap of high risk situations to avoid and helps determine the dynamics underlying the drug usage.

The importance of learning new skills cannot be expressed enough. Drugs are used as a method of coping with stress and life's challenges, often because the abuser's failure to learn proper coping techniques. In other clients, these skills may have been taught, perhaps even lived out, but their usage of drugs has negated these skills, leading to habitual drug use to cope. In still other cases, the client may have other mental problems which compound their ill use of proper coping skills.

The first few sessions in Cognitive Behavior Therapy are used to build the most basic of skills. The therapist and patient analyze high risk situations and work toward controlling and working through thoughts about cocaine (or other drug of choice). After these skills have been developed, the therapist must walk the client through socially oriented situations. These include topics such as unemployment (it can be very difficult for a drug abuser to find work) and a sense of isolation. The therapist must help the patient to bolster their self-efficacy. That is, the client must have enough confidence in themselves to refuse offers of cocaine.

Who Is This For?

The best candidates for Cognitive Behavior Therapy tend to be the average drug abuser. However, there are some specific groups who generally fail to respond to this treatment model. In particular are those who suffer from bipolar or psychotic disorders. However, if these are stabilized with medication, the therapy can be quite beneficial. CBT is also less effective with the homeless population, medically unstable and those who are dependant on multiple non-alcoholic substances.

What Format Is Best?

Individual treatment is always the preferred format to use CBT. It allows the therapist and client to work together to customize the treatment plan for individual needs. In this one-on-one model, the client is much more involved in his own treatment. It has been noted by many therapists that a patient retains much more of what they learn in one on one counsel than in a group.

On the other hand, many clinicians firmly believe that there are unique benefits to be found by delivering treatment in a group format. In most cases, CBT can be adapted to a group session, although this is not its strength. The time allotted for a meeting would have to be extended, and it would be the counselor's responsibility to insure all participants have opportunity to share their personal experiences. A distinct benefit of group treatment in conjunction with CBT is that the treatment plan can be much more structured, whereas in individual counseling the skill learning is much more personal.

When Is The Treatment Process Complete

The CBT program is offered best in 12 to 16 session treatment cycles, which are spread over a 12 - 16 week period. The reason for this quick jump start into Drug Abuse Treatment is to provide the client with an initial stabilized sense of abstinence. This, in many cases, is just what a client needs to get free of their drug. Data, which is still being tested, has shown that individuals who abstain from their drug for a three week period during their Cognitive Behavior Therapy can generally kick their drug completely within a year after treatment ends.

However, there are cases when CBT is inefficient to bring about a lasting change. In these cases, CBT may be used as preparation for a more long term treatment plan. It has been suggested that in these cases "booster sessions" of CBT for a period extending 6 months after initial treatment may be efficacious.

During these booster sessions, the therapist and client begin with several specific goals. The first is to identify situations, thought processes and events which cause the patient to lose sight of his/her abstinence. The next step is to strengthen effective coping skills which can help the client to remain free of their drug. Finally, the therapist must encourage the client to get involved with people and activities which have nothing to do with drugs. There will be activities which basically have no reference to drug use and people who are involved with drugs.

The booster form of the CBT is not to "teach" new skills. Those skills should have been taught in the initial CBT period. The purpose of the booster is to strengthen skills already learned.

Where Should CBT Sessions be Held?

In most cases, CBT is performed on an outpatient basis. This is mainly to aide the client and therapist in understanding the cause for the abuse. This, of course, is best done in the client's day to day setting. A client is more likely to display who s/he really is in a familiar environment. This allows the therapist opportunity to provide much more elaborate and functional analysis. Another reason CBT is done in this manner is because it allows the client time to practice new skills in their familiar and daily routine. The therapist can watch the client and see what works and what does not. It also allows for discussion of new strategies with the therapist.

Why CBT?

It Works! CBT is highly compatible with many other methods of treatment. When dealing with cocaine users, CBT is often used in conjunction with medication for drug related medical problems and other psychiatric disorders. CBT also works with self-help groups such as Cocaine Anonymous or Alcoholics Anonymous. In addition to these, CBT works well with Family, couples and vocational counseling. Whenever CBT is used with other methods of treatment, it is absolutely necessary that the therapist talk regularly with other providers. This can help to build new and more effective strategies for treating clients.

How CBT Is Made Up?

Cognitive Behavior Therapy is made up of both unique and common factors. Common to most all therapeutic practices found in nearly all psychotherapies include education, support, encouragement, setting goals and having the patient believe that the therapy will work for them. These principles are all found in CBT. However, unique to CBT are those techniques which stem from personal relationship with the client.

Many drug abuse therapies approach the client as a student, teaching principles, but never getting into the area of application. This will often bring a sense of alienation or boredom to the client, ultimately producing the effects contrary to the therapy's purpose. With CBT, the therapist gets to know the client. The therapist begins to see where problem issues are in the client's life and then properly develops and teaches the skills needed to cope with the specific problems.

The balance between skill training and relationship development is something that every CBT therapist should strive for. Without a good relationship, the client may not be receptive to the skills s/he needs to learn. On the other hand, with a good understanding relationship, the client may accept the skills, as from a friend, and apply them diligently to his/her life. But that balance must be reached.

In all Cognitive Behavior therapy, the therapist must analyze the client's abuse of substance in a way that is both useful for discussion and informative enough to uncover the coping skills the client needs. The therapist must never try to apply cookie cutter coping techniques to the client. These are incompatible with CBT. Instead, the therapist must train each client, as an individual, to recognize and deal with their cravings, drug related thoughts, problem solving, emergency planning, and miscellaneous decisions that, to a detached therapist, would seem irrelevant. The therapist must also build up the client so that s/he can refuse drugs when offered.

Also unique to CBT is the requirement that the therapist examine the client's thoughts related to substance abuse. This allows the therapist to make informed judgments which can lead to proper identification of past and possible future situations where drug use is likely to occur. The therapist can explain these situations to the client, walking him/her through the cognitive reasoning which has often led them to abuse drugs.

The therapist will encourage the client, building him/her up to face the real world. This gives the client a feeling that somebody believes in them. During the session, the therapist and client will practice drug-refusal and coping skills. In addition, it is expected that the therapist will review how the client used these new skills after the session was concluded.

Not CBT

Though many therapy techniques are compatible with Cognitive Behavior, there are a few which are rarely compatible, and can in some cases work against the CBT approach. One of these techniques is self-disclosure by the therapist. Though a relationship must be developed between therapist and client for CBT to work, the client rarely needs to know every intimate detail of the therapist's life.

Another technique that does not work well with CBT is confrontation. Many therapists like to jump down the client's throat whenever they step into denial. Though there are treatment techniques where this is good, it does not build a solid relational foundation between the client and therapist. Instead, it often builds a wall of rebellion.

Cognitive Behavior therapists rarely require their clients to attend self-help groups or 12-step programs. The skills that the client needs should be learned with the therapist. Though self-help groups often teach skills that can work wonders for many individuals, clients who are attending CBT sessions need to focus on the personalized skills that they receive from their sessions.

Unlike many other modes of therapy, CBT does not depend on an extensive exploration of interpersonal aspects of the client's substance abuse. Nor does it pay much attention to underlying conflicts or motives. The CBT approach also frowns on the disease model therapy and is careful not to use its disease language or slogans.

Principles of CBT

One of the most important aspects of the CBT approach to addiction counseling is the fact that it is entirely collaborative. Instead of the therapist making all of the decisions and the client following like a young child, the client is forced to make decisions and work together with the therapist. The client and therapist decide together what the goals of treatment are to be, the type of skills needed and how long this should take. This allows the therapist to work with the client, bringing an assurance that the treatment will be relevant to the client's particular needs.

Skill Learning

Skills are learned mainly through three techniques. The first is Modeling. That is, you learn by watching other people and then try to "model" their actions, hoping to achieve similar results. Young children learn to speak their native language by hearing their parents speak it. By seeing a parent abuse alcohol or smoke at an early age, children can grow up believing that these are acceptable methods of dealing with life's stressful situations.

Another method of learning is known as Operant Conditioning. This comes after an individual has performed an action, and was in some way rewarded. With drugs and alcohol, this reward can be in the form of euphoria, not feeling depressed, feeling energized and so on. Individuals will continue to act out while the promise of a reward is held out for them.

Classical Conditioning was originally described by Pavlov. He conducted an experiment with dogs, where at each meal time he would first ring a bell, and then present the dogs with their food. After a time of conditioning, the dogs would salivate even if food was absent, whenever they heard the bell ring. Pavlov was able to have the dogs salivate by simply ringing the bell. They had been conditioned to do so.

This same conditioning principle can be applied to drug abusers. It is very common for abusers of cocaine to pair events, people or things with drug use. In the past, they may have abused the drug whenever they went to certain parts of town, whenever they had money, with certain people, at certain parts of the day and so on. When these events are triggered, they can create intense cravings which are often followed by cocaine use.

Functional Analysis

A complete analysis of the client should be complete by the third session. It is here where the therapist analyzes his/her client's dependence on a substance. The first step in this process is to determine the client's personal obstacles, and perhaps any physical ailments needing attention. This includes

- Does the client realize that s/he must reduce the accessibility of his/her drug of abuse?

- Has the client recognized any drug use cues; events that trigger drug use?
- Has the client, even for a brief time, ever been able to abstain from their drug?
- Can the client identify those circumstances which often lead to relapse?
- Has the client ever successfully tolerated their cravings for their drug(s) for any amount of time, without resorting to drug use?
- Does the client understand that there is a relationship between other drugs of abuse with their main drug… (i.e. alcohol).
- Does the client have any psychiatric problems which might get in the way of attempts to change behavior?

After you determine what deficiencies your client may have, it is time to outline what skills and strengths the client has. These will be very important as you attempt to teach the user new skills.

- What skills has the client demonstrated during past times of abstinence?
- Has the client been able to stay in a positive relationship or keep a job while abusing drugs?
- Does the client have any friends, co-workers, etc. who do neither take nor sell drugs?
- Does the client know anyone who can bolster his/her effort to remain abstinent?
- What are some non-drug-related things the client does?
- What was the client highest level of function before introduction to drugs?
- Why is the client in treatment now?
- How much motivation does the client exert towards abstinence?

Finally, the therapist must have an understanding of what events trigger the client's drug use. These are known as determinants of drug use.

- What is the client usual pattern of use (i.e. do they take it on the weekends, each day, 3rd Tuesdays of each month, or binge use)?
- What events, objects, people, etc., trigger the client craving for their drug?
- Does the client generally use drugs with other people, or all alone?
- In what specific locations does the client buy and use their drug?
- How does the client get the money to pay for drugs?

- What events surround the times when drug abuse became problematic?
- What roles (good and bad) has the client's drug use played in his/her life?

In order to identify these determinants, the therapist should also focus on the following five general life domains: Social, Environmental, Emotional, Cognitive and Physical.

Skill Teaching

One of the primary goals of Cognitive Behavior Therapy is the teaching of new positive skills and the "un-learning" of negative ones. Drug abuse is a skill! It is a complex skill, bringing with it a set of other skills. For instance, the drug user has usually learned skills for getting the money to pay for their drugs, how to acquire drugs without being caught, and use their drugs without being "found out."

As discussed earlier, people learn new skills by modeling others, by Operant Conditioning and by conditioning similar to that of Pavlov's. Because the CBT program is generally brief, most of the skills learned bust be fairly general. These skills are taught with the hope that the client will gain control over their substances of abuse. However, it is important that the client, and therapist, understand that these skills can be applied to other areas of life, not just drug abuse. Problem solving skills can be applied to just about any life situation.

A therapist involved in CBT should pay very close attention to the skills being taught. There are some guidelines to follow which have been shown to be most effective. First of all, make sure that the basic skills are taught first. During the therapy process, it is best to start with the skills which address issues of craving for the drug, motivation to discontinue drug use, and other skills which help the client deal with the constant availability of drugs.

Once the fundamental skills have been learned, the therapist may build on these. Later sessions may be dedicated to problem solving or subtle mental mindsets. The skills that the client receives in relation to controlling their desire for drugs can be used as a foundation for teaching them how to manage thought processes which often lead to drug use.

Another guideline that therapists should use while teaching their clients new skills is that the material must be applicable to the client's needs.

Because CBT is highly individualized, the therapist cannot resort to a cookbook mentality, where a client's need receives a predefined skill. Instead, all the skills which must be learned are custom tailored to each client's individual needs. This requires that the therapist and client collaborate, making therapy decisions together. Successful treatment often requires some creativity as well.

In order to make skills applicable to the client, the therapist MUST provide examples. These stories need to be relevant to the client's needs. It is often easiest to use the client's own history. For example, if the client used drugs between sessions, you might want to talk about the events surrounding that, and work your skill building into the dialogue.

Repetition is perhaps the best method of establishing and rooting a particular skill in an individual. Unfortunately, many clients who come seeking treatment have been using their drug for so long it has become second nature. It is thoroughly moored in their subconscious as their "normal" lifestyle. In order to counter this, the therapist must also use repetition, especially during the early sessions. This means teaching the same skills with many different examples and applications so that the client grabs onto these stories, learning the principles that they contain.

Another guideline that therapists must follow is the concept of skill mastery. That is, the client must not only see the skills modeled, or have them lectured, the client must practice them him/herself. On occasion the patient will make mistakes. When these occur, the therapist must assure the client that s/he is not a failure, and that the mistake can be learned from. This is how skills are mastered. Without an occasional mistake, there is no way to assure that the client will be able to handle the "inevitable" mistakes down the road.

To practice skills, the client and therapist can walk through exercises such as role playing, story telling and so on. The therapist should exert a bit of creativity in this area. The more action, the greater the cognitive imprint. For each session, it is also important that homework be assigned to the client. These exercises are designed to allow the client to safely test new behaviors and recognize their value.

Strategic Skill Teaching

In order to encourage the client to practice the skills learned during each session, there are several strategies you may follow.

The first is to make sure the client understands the value of a particular skill. A therapist should not expect anyone to blindly practice new behaviors or do extra-session homework without an understanding why it might be helpful. The therapist must clearly explain why the client needs to practice the particular skill, and the benefits of compliance.

Another strategy is to obtain a commitment. This means that the therapist must actually ask the client whether s/he would be willing to practice skills outside the session. We all are more willing to do things once we have given our word. Until you have a clear "yes" you do not have a commitment. Hesitation or refusal can also be seen as helpful hints as to where the patient is in the development process, and what special needs s/he might need. It may be that the client does not want to do the homework because s/he does not understand its value.

As the therapist closes the session, it is important to reiterate the different steps involved with their "homework." The client must be given the opportunity to ask questions, and give input. This will not only help them learn the skills, but will also give you another opportunity to gauge their progress. Follow up is also an essential tool to the therapist, and ultimately to the client. It is the therapist's duty to make sure that the client is actually completing his/her homework. Whenever a task is discussed in a particular meeting, make sure to bring it up in the following session.

It is true that many clients will fail to complete their weekly homework, while others will actually do their homework in the waiting room before the session. This resistance signifies that the client has doubts as to their ability to handle a drug free life. It is the therapist's job to find out the source of the client's resistance against following through with the tasks given. By determining why the client does not do the prescribed homework, you can help them to work through their problems.

Encouraging the client is very important. The therapist must be very watchful for any positive information the client gives. Whenever a client provides an insight, or in any way completes a task, this should be reward; especially during the early stages of treatment. Praise should always be followed with a reiteration of the importance of practice.

Session Flow

Each CBT session should run about an hour. This hour is generally divided into 3 twenty minute segments (also known as the 20/20/20 rule).

The first part of the session assesses the client's experiences with drugs since the last session. This should include a drug test. The therapist should ask the client about any interaction with drugs and situations that might have led to drug abuse. If the drug test reveals that the client has used drugs, and they have said that there was no drug use, this should be discussed as well. As the therapist and client talk about the time between sessions, the therapist must pay special attention to the client's concerns and thoughts about the treatment.

The second part of the session is a time of teaching. First of all, the topic for the session must be taught. First the topic is introduced in general terms. The client and therapist discuss the new skill. In order to assure that the client understands the relevance of the skill, the client must also relate the skill to the client's current problems and challenges. Finally, the therapist must look for reactions from the client. You need to ask the client to relate specific times when the new skill would have been particularly useful. Role playing is also a useful method of gauging the client's understanding of the session's topic.

The final third of the session is very similar to the first. The client does most of the talking while the therapist listens and guides the discussion by questions and asking for clarification of ideas. This is also the time when the client's homework is assigned. During this time, the therapist should be able to outline what high risk situations the patient will be facing in the following week, and should base the homework exercises accordingly.

Skills and Topics

The CBT program is divided into 8 major themes, while it usually runs 12-16 weeks. This is done to afford the therapist room for personalization of the material. Some clients may need more than one session to learn a particular skill, while other individuals can master a skill very quickly. In addition to the 8 topics provided by the basic CBT program, there are also additional topics which are not applicable to many drug users.

The first session is the most important. This is the time when the therapist must establish a relationship with the client. The therapist must also assess the level of addiction, substance use and other problems that may factor into the treatment process. During this session, the therapist must also outline the rationale for the treatment, establishing a process to follow for the remaining sessions. Also, this is a good time to begin the skill teaching process. Due to the vast amount of territory to cover in this first session, it

154

is a good idea to set aside at least 90 minutes.

Following the first session, it is time to start teaching the main topics of the CBT plan. The first of these is:

Coping With Craving. The therapist must give the client an understanding of craving, which often includes information as to where this craving originates. The client must describe their cravings and identify what triggers these cravings. The therapist should have questions prepared to focus in on these triggers. These questions should cover the five areas discussed earlier: Social, Environmental, Emotional, Cognitive and Physical.

Once the therapist and client have an understanding of the craving's source, they must start working on plans to avoid these triggers. Some of the common methods of doing this include getting rid of drug abuse paraphernalia, avoiding drug users and staying away from areas where drugs were used previously.

The client must learn the skill of recognizing their drug craving triggers, avoiding them, and coping with the craving. Coping can be accomplished in several ways: distraction, talking about the craving, letting the craving pass, recalling the negative effects of previous drug use and self-talk.

The next CBT topic is **Shoring Up Motivation and Commitment to Stop**. At this point, the therapist has conducted several functional analyses, and should therefore have a clear understanding of where the client is heading. The sessions which discuss this topic include skills such as clarifying and prioritizing goals and addressing ambivalence. Without a goal to strive for, the client will often feel helpless, like their efforts are worthless.

Also, this topic deals with identifying and coping with thoughts regarding drug use. The therapist understands that the leading 'trigger' back into drug usage is drug related thinking. Some of the more common (and erroneous) thoughts include:

- I can be around friends who use drugs without using.
- I love being high.
- Nothing has worked in the past, I might as well not try quitting.
- I deserve a reward.
- I failed again, I might as well get high.

These thoughts must be avoided at all costs. Some clients find this to be a very difficult task, but there are methods which have been shown to take the focus off of drug related thoughts. One such method is to think about one's goals in life. During those sessions which cover this topic, the therapist should have the client go over their short-term and long-term goals. These should be as concrete as possible; not wishes and dreams, but real workable goals.

Some of the other methods for coping with thoughts about drug abuse include:

- Thinking past the high and focusing on the downside. Clients should focus on a particularly bad experience. This can be a powerful deterrent to further use.
- Challenge the thoughts. That is, the client should think of reasons why not using drugs is so important (i.e. "It is much more important to keep my family together.").
- Review negative consequences
- Distraction. These should include activities which can be done at any time, during any kind of weather and should be enjoyable. Not all distractions should rely on others.
- Talking.

The third topic covers **Refusal Skills and Assertiveness**. This is a major issue for many drug users. Those clients who experience ambivalence in relation to their therapy often have great difficulty refusing drugs when they are directly offered them. It is often true that the social networks of drug abuse clients are very narrow, including only people who are in some way involved with drugs. Some clients have gotten themselves so enmeshed in their drug use networks that getting out can be difficult.

The main skills being taught with this topic include assessing the availability of the client's drugs of abuse and what steps could be taken to reduce this availability. The therapist and client must discuss strategies for breaking contacts with those people who have been supplying drugs in the past. Accomplishing this task is often very difficult, and not always possible. For instance, it is common for clients to be married to a partner who uses cocaine. In this case, limiting exposure to drugs, or keeping them out of the house might be a solution. The therapist and client must work these details out together.

A very important skill is that of drug refusal skills. The basic principle of a good refusal technique is firstly to respond quickly. There can be no hesitation. Good eye contact is a key to this skill. A firm "no" which leaves no door open for future offers should suffice.

The fourth topic covers **Irrelevant Decisions**. The therapist walks the client through their seemingly irrelevant decisions and how these have a direct relationship with high-risk situations. In order to make sure the client fully understands, the therapist will discuss examples of past times when they "accidentally" took drugs. The therapist will walk the client through the events of that day, looking for any decisions which led to drug use. Some of the most common "irrelevant decisions" include things like:

- Drinking alcohol
- Having alcohol in the house
- Keeping drug use paraphernalia
- Going places where drugs are commonly abused
- Interacting with drug abusers
- Not telling family members about past drug use
- Not telling old drug-using associates of their decision to quit
- Not making plans to be continually busy.

An **All-Purpose Coping Plan** is the fifth topic for discussion between the therapist and client. Often times, even when the client is determined to quit and has put forth every effort to do stay free of high-risk situations, these still come up. Examples of these triggers include losing a job, being diagnosed with HIV (always a risk for drug abusers) or losing a loved one. Positive events can also act as high-risk triggers as well. These positives can include getting a large sum of money at one time or starting out in a new intimate relationship. Because these events can occur at any time, and they come with little warning, it is always best to be prepared with an emergency coping plan.

The skills learned from the All-Purpose Coping Plan include the ability to anticipate high-risk situations as well as developing a personal coping plan which is generic enough to be applicable to just about every situation. The therapist is to ask the client to look ahead into the future and pinpoint three or four major sources of stress which might arise during that time. Then the therapist is to ask the client what possible stresses could shake their commitment to abstinence from drugs. The patient and client should develop concrete coping plans for these possible events.

The generic coping technique should be just that, generic. It should require no special events, or special circumstances. At a minimum, this coping plan should include a set of phone numbers that the client can call for support. These people need to be reliable. This plan should also have the client recall the negative consequences of returning to drug use as well as positive thoughts which can be substituted for any high-risk drug thoughts. Things which distract the client from thinking about drugs should also be included in this plan. Finally, the client should have a list of safe places which are free of temptations that s/he can go to wait out the crisis.

The sixth session topic is **Problem Solving**. The main skills taught under this topic include the introduction to basic concepts of problem solving and having the client practice these problem solving skills with the therapist. It is unfortunate that so many drug users have come to look on their substance of abuse as their primary means of coping with life's problems. This topic explains the process of problem solving as follows:

- Recognize that there is a problem
- Identify and specify the Problem
- Consider various approaches to solving the problem (various means more than 2)
- Select the approach with the best final outcome
- Assess the effectiveness of that approach.

During any sessions dealing with this topic, the therapist must make it clear that some problems will be easy to solve, while others will be much more difficult. The therapist will also test the patient with hypothetical situations and examples from the patient's own history. The therapist should point out the strengths of the patient's approach to problem solving, and should provide understandable instruction for improvement.

Nearing the end of the CBT program comes **Case Management**, the seventh topic for discussion. This topic has to do with the client's ability to plan and make goals in the real world. The client and therapist must work together, reviewing and applying problem solving skills to real world problems which may become a barrier to final treatment. The therapist and client must also work together building a solid support plan which addresses these problems. To do this, the client's life goals will be laid out, and plans for achievement will be enacted. The therapist will guide the client to whatever social-service systems s/he needs to contact to build around their goals.

From session to session, the therapist will question the client as to whether s/he acted on these plans. If the client is moving forward in their goals, the therapist is to provide praise. Even the smallest steps are significant! The therapist should show the client that they are confident in his/her ability to succeed and to acquire whatever services are needed. The main purpose of this segment of the Cognitive Behavior Therapy plan is to build up the client's level of self-efficacy.

The final topic in the CBT program is **HIV Risk Reduction**. Generally speaking, it is rare for an individual to get HIV from taking cocaine or other syringe related drugs because of particular safety precautions. However, those who do abuse drugs, often also abuse their bodies through unsafe sexual practices. It is not uncommon for a recovering cocaine user to admit having had many sexual partners during their time of drug use.

This purpose of this topic is to assess the client's risk of HIV. It is also designed to teach the client the problem solving skills necessary to overcome barriers to HIV risk reduction goals. The therapist will share information on how the patient can lower his/her risk with some of the following pointers:

- Of course, abstinence is the ONLY 100% method to avoid the sexual transmission of HIV and other sexually transmitted diseases.
- Making sure the client understands the concept of harm reduction versus abstinence
- The client should understand the methods of transmission
- The client should be acquainted with the dangers of sharing drug injection equipment and proper cleaning procedures

The final session is a time of saying good bye. The therapist and client look back over their course of treatment, reviewing the plans and goals set together. The client should get feedback from the therapist in regards to his/her progress in the treatment. At the same time, the therapist should seek the client's feedback on the most helpful parts of the program, as well as those areas which did not seem as useful.

In some cases, especially when the client has failed to maintain abstinence, it is a good idea to suggest that the client seek further treatment in a clinical program, in-patient or a day treatment facility.

Conclusion

This chapter has shown how the CBT program can be utilized in the counselor's office to aide those suffering from Substance Addiction. In tests where CBT was placed side by side with other treatment programs, CBT either came out even, or came out ahead. The primary strength of CBT is the giving of skills to the client. Even when relapses do occur after treatment, the client is much more likely to continue to improve, using the skills they have learned in treatment. Once new problem solving and coping skills have been built into a client's mindset, it is difficult for them to go wholly back to their drugs of addiction as a way of escape. They have learned a new way.

Chapter Twelve Questions for Discussion

1. What is CBT?

2. Who are the best candidates for CBT?

3. Why should CBT be performed on an out-patient basis?

4. Skills are learned mainly through what three techniques?

5. To practice skills, the patient and therapist can walk through what kinds of exercises?

6. Describe the 20/20/20 rule.

7. What are the eight main topics of the CBT plan?

8. What is the primary strength of CBT versus other programs?

Addendum One

An Assessment

This is an assessment of an actual client, which should help us to visualize the process of assessing a client. Take a good look at the information included and note the detail that it contains.

Patient Identification:

Frank[11] is a 29 year old Caucasian male. He is slightly overweight, with a curly beard. He presents himself as a reasonably intelligent and articulate young man, although he has no close friends. Frank has been a mechanic, working off and on with various specialty cars and has lived at home for all of his life until the incident that brought him in for treatment.

Source of referral:

Frank is a private placement, encouraged by his parents in lieu of going to court. He was placed due to aggressive, out of control behavior, which was partially due to his drug involvement and partially due to some apparent but serious psychological difficulties.

Present problem:

Frank was referred for treatment due to drug and alcohol abuse and serious aggressive behavior toward his parents. Just before treatment he became violent toward his mother, who has been his primary support. Frank has never been on his own, and is an overly dependent young man. He is especially dependent his mother. At the time of his removal from the home, there was extensive fragmentation of his sense of self and self-esteem.

---

[11] Names and situations have been altered for purposes of confidentiality. However, the case represented is real.

Prior treatment and hospitalization:

Just prior to placement at this Center for Addictive Services, Frank was briefly admitted to a mental hospital where he was evaluated for drug, alcohol and psychiatric difficulties. While at the hospital, he was placed on some medications: Haldol and Cogentin. He is no longer on the medication. There was no other prior medical treatment of the problem.

Social relationships:

Frank's social relationships are limited. He likes being with people, and yet avoids fully connecting with them. If he had his druthers he would be at home working on a car. Home is a "safe place" where he does not have to deal with relationships.

Recreation and leisure time:

Most of his time is either spent working on his car, driving his car, occasionally using some substance and riding his bicycle on the Boardwalk. Increasingly, Frank relates that he could ride his bike up and down the Boardwalk at the beach, day after day after day, without making contact with people and feel most content.

Education:

Frank was a 4.0 student through High School and was a 4.0 student in his first two years of Junior College. He emphasized mechanics and especially the maintenance and repair of automobiles during his junior college tenure. At this point, he has no ambition for further education.

Employment history:

Most of his employment has been working with various mechanic's shops throughout the county, and as a contractor doing specialized work as required on Porsches. He says, "If you're going to work on cars, you might as well work on the best." Auto repair seems to be his only love and true interest in life.

History of Substance Abuse:

Frank began drinking for the first time in 1979 and has averaged a six pack of beer a day. He relates that he quit two years ago in 1986. Further, he started smoking marijuana in 1979 and described it as part of his religion. He doesn't think that it is a problem. However, he recently stopped because it was getting him into some trouble. In 1985, he began using crystal methamphetamine. He just stopped using approximately three weeks ago, prior to his explosion and entering the treatment center.

Mental Status Exam:

Frank is oriented to time, place and person. However, he does exhibit some forms of fantasy defense, loose association, and some ideas of reference in his thought processes. He also exhibits some paranoiac thought processes. He is, however, able to make verbal and emotional contact. He does have modulation in his thought processes and sometimes inappropriate humor. It is my assumption that this is related to both the drug usage as well as schizoid personality characteristics.

Clinical evaluation:

Frank has clear signs of severe psychological stress. His entering the treatment facility and the separation from his family has been difficult. Frank is not particularly depressed, but is, in fact quite cheerful, outgoing, and active. This may also indicate that he is rather self-seeking, and perhaps lacks appropriate social judgment. Further, Frank is easily agitated and can act impulsively with significant anger. At the same time, he has the ability to be self-aware, has concern for social issues, and can be quite introspective. This is something we hope to capitalize on through the treatment process. Further, Frank is interpersonally sensitive to the way people see him. He is highly sensitive to criticism and tends to personalize the actions of others towards himself. He is also worried, tense, indecisive, has significant anxiety and becomes agitated when things do not go the way he wishes. A most important note is that Frank scored very high on scale eight of the MMPI. This is from the Minnesota Multiphasic Personality Inventory. This may indicate that Frank feels alienated and remote from his environment, which is primarily due to situational and personal distress.

Although his mood is typically positive, he can easily and quickly become negative. He is impulsive, yet has an ability to delay gratification. Socially, he is rather withdrawn and has a difficult time relating to others. He was bonded, primarily to his mother, and secondarily to his father. He is like a young boy that can not leave his mother. He has been so significantly tied in with her that he is unable to process through the separation and individuation.

Recommended treatment:

First of all, Frank needs to stabilize with the Center for Addictive Services and attend their 28 day treatment program. Since detoxification has occurred during his time in county jail, general treatment can commence. Secondly, he will need to attend all classes and groups to learn more about the addictive process. Thirdly, Frank will require intensive and supportive CBT oriented psychotherapy with the intention of helping him cope with his underlying fear of abandonment, which has been brought to the forefront because of his separation from mother and father. Finally, Frank is going to need significant aftercare services to insure that he doesn't fall back into the same patterns of behavior as before.

Respectfully submitted

Stan E. DeKoven Ph.D. MF Counselor

The only details of this assessment that have been altered are the names. When you do your assessments, you will need to remember to keep them completely confidential. That report is for your eyes only, unless subpoenaed by a court of law.

Addendum Two

Exercise in Assessment

Following is an exercise which will give you a good look into the counseling process. It would be best if you had a partner to do this with, but if you have none, then you will have to do your best. This exercise is divided into two parts, both of which are equally important and are to be done by each partner separately.

Part one:

In this exercise you will write a fictitious assessment on a fictitious client. You can present the client any way you want so long as they have a substance abuse problem. You need to retain the humanity of your fictitious individual and try to make him/her as real as possible. Use your imagination and create something original. You may actually find something out about yourself as you do this assignment.

If your imagination is not as strong as this project may require, then you are allowed to use a real person and write an assessment on them, but in respect for them, change their name, address, etc.

On your evaluation, you will need to follow the basic formula for assessment that is provided. Include all of the pertinent information that you have read about. Follow the format and layout provided, with as much detail as possible.

Patient Identification:

Source of referral:

Present problem:

Prior treatment and hospitalization:

Social relationships:

Recreation and leisure time:

Education:

Employment history: History of Substance Abuse:

Mental Status Exam:

Clinical evaluation:

Recommended treatment:

Summary

Part two:

This is where having a partner can be essential for the purpose of the assignment. Your partner will also have written one of these evaluations, and you will trade. You will each read the other's evaluation, and attempt

168

to come up with alternative or additional treatment strategies.

Your method of treatment should be as in-depth as you can possibly make it. You can do whatever you want to treat the client, but keep it within the scope of the book and support materials. Think of the evaluation as a real person and focus on what you would really do if a person with a similar background were to walk into your office and say, "I need help."

As the writer of the treatment plan, you will need to answer some very important questions. Discuss your long range plans for the treatment of the individual, and why

Note:

When writing your evaluation(s), give as much information as possible. Give your partner a good case history to work with so that they can have as much fun writing the treatment plan as you did creating the dysfunctional person.

Remember, this is not an examination or test, but it is a genuine exercise designed to increase your clinical experience. It will prepare you for actual practice.

Addendum Three

Stages of Development
Eight Stages of Man

Stage	Issues	Summary
I. Oral Sensory 0-2	Basis Trust vs. Mistrust	In this stage, it is essential for individuals to form a sense of basic trust in their caregivers and in their environment.
II. Muscular Anal	Autonomy vs. Shame Doubt	In this stage, a child must have a clear understanding of his/her boundaries. This fosters a sense of self-control.
III. Locomotor Genital 2-5	Initiative vs. Guilt	During this time, a child is reaching out to master his/her environment. Children learn skills such as goal setting in this stage. Overcorrecting may lead to a sense of guilt.
IV. Latency 6-12	Industry vs. Inferiority	This is a time when a child learns to harness his/her imagination. They strive to meet goals and earn rewards. A child may think himself inferior to others if there in neglect, abuse or similar problems in the home.
V. Puberty and Adolescence 12-18	Identity vs. Role Confusion	At this stage, an individual begins learning who they are and their role in society.

VI. Young Adulthood 19-35	Intimacy vs. Isolation	This stage brings with it a more solidified sense of identity as the individual begins various types of relationships with others.
VII. Adulthood 35-65	Generativity vs. Stagnation	During this stage, individuals look back to evaluate their life's worth – to see what they are generating. These individuals desire to share their knowledge with upcoming generations.
VIII. Maturity Over 65	Ego Integrity vs. Despair	At this time, an individual begins to take one of two outlooks on life: Those who accept the first view, hold to a sense of completion in their life.

Addendum Four
Commonly Abused Drugs

Substance: Category and Name	Examples of *Commercial* and Street Names	DEA Schedule*/ How Administered**	*Intoxication Effects*/Potential Health Consequences
Cannabinoids			*euphoria, slowed thinking and reaction time, confusion, impaired balance and coordination*/cough, frequent respiratory infections; impaired memory and learning; increased heart rate, anxiety; panic attacks; tolerance, addiction
hashish	boom, chronic, gangster, hash, hash oil, hemp	I/swallowed, smoked	
marijuana	blunt, dope, ganja, grass, herb, joints, Mary Jane, pot, reefer, sinsemilla, skunk, weed	I/swallowed, smoked	
Depressants			*reduced anxiety; feeling of well-being; lowered inhibitions; slowed pulse and breathing; lowered blood pressure; poor concentration*/fatigue; confusion; impaired coordination, memory, judgment; addiction; respiratory depression and arrest, death
barbiturates	*Amytal, Nembutal, Seconal, Phenobarbital;* barbs, reds, red birds, phennies, tooies, yellows, yellow jackets	II, III, V/injected, swallowed	
benzodiazepines (other than flunitrazepam)	*Ativan, Halcion, Librium, Valium, Xanax;* candy, downers, sleeping pills, tranks	IV/swallowed, injected	*Also, for barbiturates—sedation, drowsiness*/depression, unusual excitement, fever, irritability, poor judgment, slurred speech, dizziness, life-threatening withdrawal.
flunitrazepam***	*Rohypnol;* forget-me pill, Mexican Valium, R2, Roche, roofies, roofinol, rope, rophies	IV/swallowed, snorted	*for benzodiazepines—sedation, drowsiness*/dizziness
GHB***	*gamma-hydroxybutyrate;* G, Georgia home boy, grievous bodily harm, liquid ecstasy	I/swallowed	*for flunitrazepam—visual and gastrointestinal disturbances, urinary retention, memory loss for the time under the drug's effects*
methaqualone	*Quaalude, Sopor, Parest;* ludes, mandrex, quad, quay	I/injected, swallowed	*for GHB—drowsiness, nausea*/vomiting, headache, loss of consciousness, loss of reflexes, seizures, coma, death
			for methaqualone—euphoria/depression, poor reflexes, slurred speech, coma
Dissociative Anesthetics			*increased heart rate and blood pressure, impaired motor function*/memory loss; numbness; nausea/vomiting
ketamine	*Ketalar SV;* cat Valiums, K, Special K, vitamin K	III/injected, snorted, smoked	
PCP and analogs	*phencyclidine;* angel dust, boat, hog, love boat, peace pill	I, II/injected, swallowed, smoked	*Also, for ketamine—at high doses, delirium, depression, respiratory depression and arrest*

			for PCP and analogs—possible decrease in blood pressure and heart rate, panic, aggression, violence/loss of appetite, depression
Hallucinogens			altered states of perception and feeling; nausea; persisting perception disorder (flashbacks)
LSD	*lysergic acid diethylamide;* acid, blotter, boomers, cubes, microdot, yellow sunshines	I/swallowed, absorbed through mouth tissues	*Also, for LSD and mescaline—* increased body temperature, heart rate, blood pressure; loss of appetite, sleeplessness, numbness, weakness, tremors
mescaline	buttons, cactus, mesc, peyote	I/swallowed, smoked	
psilocybin	magic mushroom, purple passion, shrooms	I/swallowed	*for LSD —persistent mental disorders* *for psilocybin—nervousness, paranoia*

Opioids and Morphine Derivatives			
codeine	*Empirin with Codeine, Fiorinal with Codeine, Robitussin A-C, Tylenol with Codeine;* Captain Cody, Cody, schoolboy; (with glutethimide) doors & fours, loads, pancakes and syrup	II, III, IV/injected, swallowed	pain relief, euphoria, drowsiness/nausea, constipation, confusion, sedation, respiratory depression and arrest, tolerance, addiction, unconsciousness, coma, death
fentanyl and fentanyl analogs	*Actiq, Duragesic, Sublimaze;* Apache, China girl, China white, dance fever, friend, goodfella, jackpot, murder 8, TNT, Tango and Cash	I, II/injected, smoked, snorted	*Also, for codeine—less analgesia, sedation, and respiratory depression than morphine* *for heroin—staggering gait*
heroin	*diacetylmorphine;* brown sugar, dope, H, horse, junk, skag, skunk, smack, white horse	I/injected, smoked, snorted	
morphine	*Roxanol, Duramorph;* M, Miss Emma, monkey, white stuff	II, III/injected, swallowed, smoked	
opium	*laudanum, paregoric;* big O, black stuff, block, gum, hop	II, III, V/swallowed, smoked	
oxycodone HCL	*Oxycontin;* Oxy, O.C., killer	II/swallowed, snorted, injected	
hydrocodone bitartrate, acetaminophen	*Vicodin;* vike, Watson-387	II/swallowed	
Stimulants			increased heart rate, blood pressure, metabolism;
amphetamine	*Biphetamine,*	II/injected,	

173

	Dexedrine; bennies, black beauties, crosses, hearts, LA turnaround, speed, truck drivers, uppers	swallowed, smoked, snorted	*feelings of exhilaration, energy, increased mental alertness*/rapid or irregular heart beat; reduced appetite, weight loss, heart failure, nervousness, insomnia
cocaine	*Cocaine hydrochloride;* blow, bump, C, candy, Charlie, coke, crack, flake, rock, snow, toot	II/injected, smoked, snorted	*Also, for amphetamine— rapid breathing*/ tremor, loss of coordination; irritability, anxiousness, restlessness, delirium, panic, paranoia, impulsive behavior, aggressiveness, tolerance, addiction, psychosis
MDMA (methylenedioxy- methamphetamine)	Adam, clarity, ecstasy, Eve, lover's speed, peace, STP, X, XTC	I/swallowed	
methamphetamine	*Desoxyn;* chalk, crank, crystal, fire, glass, go fast, ice, meth, speed	II/injected, swallowed, smoked, snorted	
methylphenidate (safe and effective for treatment of ADHD)	*Ritalin;* JIF, MPH, R-ball, Skippy, the smart drug, vitamin R	II/injected, swallowed, snorted	*for cocaine—increased temperature*/chest pain, respiratory failure, nausea, abdominal pain, strokes, seizures, headaches, malnutrition, panic attacks
nicotine	cigarettes, cigars, smokeless tobacco, snuff, spit tobacco, bidis, chew	not scheduled/smoked, snorted, taken in snuff and spit tobacco	*for MDMA—mild hallucinogenic effects, increased tactile sensitivity, empathic feelings*/impaired memory and learning, hyperthermia, cardiac toxicity, renal failure, liver toxicity

for methamphetamine— aggression, violence, psychotic behavior/memory loss, cardiac and neurological damage; impaired memory and learning, tolerance, addiction

*for nicotine—additional effects attributable to tobacco exposure, adverse pregnancy outcomes, chronic lung disease, cardiovascular disease, stroke, cancer, tolerance, addiction |

Other Compounds			
anabolic steroids	*Anadrol, Oxandrin, Durabolin, Depo- Testosterone, Equipoise;* roids, juice	III/injected, swallowed, applied to skin	*no intoxication effects*/hypertension, blood clotting and cholesterol changes, liver cysts and cancer, kidney cancer, hostility and aggression, acne; in adolescents, premature stoppage of growth; in males, prostate cancer, reduced sperm production, shrunken testicles, breast enlargement; in females, menstrual irregularities, development of beard and other masculine characteristics

174

| inhalants | Solvents (paint thinners, gasoline, glues), gases (butane, propane, aerosol propellants, nitrous oxide), nitrites (isoamyl, isobutyl, cyclohexyl); laughing gas, poppers, snappers, whippets | not scheduled/inhaled through nose or mouth | stimulation, loss of inhibition; headache; nausea or vomiting; slurred speech, loss of motor coordination; wheezing/unconsciousness, cramps, weight loss, muscle weakness, depression, memory impairment, damage to cardiovascular and nervous systems, sudden death |

*Schedule I and II drugs have a high potential for abuse. They require greater storage security and have a quota on manufacturing, among other restrictions. Schedule I drugs are available for research only and have no approved medical use; Schedule II drugs are available only by prescription (unrefillable) and require a form for ordering. Schedule III and IV drugs are available by prescription, may have five refills in 6 months, and may be ordered orally. Most Schedule V drugs are available over the counter.

**Taking drugs by injection can increase the risk of infection through needle contamination with staphylococci, HIV, hepatitis, and other organisms.

***Associated with sexual assaults.

Principles of Drug Addiction Treatment

Nearly three decades of scientific research has yielded 13 fundamental principles that characterize effective drug abuse treatment. These principles are detailed in <u>NIDA's Principles of Drug Addiction Treatment: A Research-Based Guide</u>.

1. **No single treatment is appropriate for all individuals.** Matching treatment settings, interventions, and services to each patient's problems and needs is critical.

2. **Treatment needs to be readily available.** Treatment applicants can be lost if treatment is not immediately available or readily accessible.

3. **Effective treatment attends to multiple needs of the individual, not just his or her drug use.** Treatment must address the individual's drug use and associated medical, psychological, social, vocational, and legal problems.

4. **At different times during treatment, a patient may develop a**

need for medical services, family therapy, vocational rehabilitation, and social and legal services.

5. **Remaining in treatment for an adequate period of time is critical for treatment effectiveness.** The time depends on an individual's needs. For most patients, the threshold of significant improvement is reached at about 3 months in treatment. Additional treatment can produce further progress. Programs should include strategies to prevent patients from leaving treatment prematurely.

6. **Individual and/or group counseling and other behavioral therapies are critical components of effective treatment for addiction.** In therapy, patients address motivation, build skills to resist drug use, replace drug-using activities with constructive and rewarding nondrug-using activities, and improve problem-solving abilities. Behavioral therapy also facilitates interpersonal relationships.

7. **Medications are an important element of treatment for many patients, especially when combined with counseling and other behavioral therapies.** Methadone and levo-alpha-acetylmethodol (LAAM) help persons addicted to opiates stabilize their lives and reduce their drug use. Naltrexone is effective for some opiate addicts and some patients with co-occurring alcohol dependence. Nicotine patches or gum, or an oral medication, such as buproprion, can help persons addicted to nicotine.

8. **Addicted or drug-abusing individuals with coexisting mental disorders should have both disorders treated in an integrated way.**

9. **Medical detoxification is only the first stage of addiction treatment and by itself does little to change long-term drug use.** Medical detoxification manages the acute physical symptoms of withdrawal. For some individuals it is a precursor to effective drug addiction treatment.

10. **Treatment does not need to be voluntary to be effective.** Sanctions or enticements in the family, employment setting, or criminal justice system can significantly increase treatment entry, retention, and success.

11. **Possible drug use during treatment must be monitored**

176

continuously. Monitoring a patient's drug and alcohol use during treatment, such as through urinalysis, can help the patient withstand urges to use drugs. Such monitoring also can provide early evidence of drug use so that treatment can be adjusted.

12. **Treatment programs should provide assessment for HIV/AIDS, hepatitis B and C, tuberculosis and other infectious diseases, and counseling to help patients modify or change behaviors that place them or others at risk of infection.** Counseling can help patients avoid high-risk behavior and help people who are already infected manage their illness.

13. **Recovery from drug addiction can be a long-term process and frequently requires multiple episodes of treatment.** As with other chronic illnesses, relapses to drug use can occur during or after successful treatment episodes. Participation in self-help support programs during and following treatment often helps maintain abstinence.

Words Defined

Abstinence – *Abstinence* implies the willful avoidance of pleasures, especially of food and drink, thought to be harmful or self-indulgent

AA, *NAS* or *ACA* – A nonprofit voluntary self-help organization of current and former alcoholics/drug abusers whose aim is to help themselves and others overcome their problem of alcoholism/drug abuse.

Amnesia - Partial or total loss of memory, usually resulting from shock, psychological disturbance, brain injury, or illness.

Assessment – the process to determine possible causes of psychological/behavioral problems

Avoidance - The act of avoiding or shunning; keeping clear of. ``The avoidance of pain." --Beattie.

Boundaries – Knowing where one person in a relationship stops and another begins. The ability to establish healthy closeness and distance between people.

Co-dependent - Of or relating to a relationship in which one person is psychologically dependent in an unhealthy way on someone who is addicted to a drug or self-destructive behavior, such as chronic gambling.

Compulsive - Caused or conditioned by compulsion or obsession. An urge to perform an act or ritualized series of acts which if not completed leads to intolerable anxiety.

Conditioning - A process of behavior modification by which a subject comes to associate a desired behavior with a previously unrelated stimulus.

Denial - An unconscious defense mechanism characterized by refusal to acknowledge painful realities, thoughts, or feelings.

Developmental – the process of growth from conception to death; specifically the study of various stages of growth from birth to grave.

Dysfunctional - Abnormal or impaired functioning, especially of a bodily system or social group.

Ego - The self, especially as distinct from the world and other selves. In psychoanalysis, the division of the psyche that is conscious, most immediately controls thought and behavior, and is most in touch with external reality.

Enmeshment - To entangle or be overly involved in other people's lives.

Family system - A fundamental social group in society typically consisting of one or two parents and their children.

Family trauma - An event or situation that causes great distress and disruption within the family.

Habituation - The decline of a conditioned response following repeated exposure to the conditioned stimulus. Physiological tolerance to a drug resulting from repeated use; psychological dependence on a drug.

Homeostasis - The ability or tendency of an organism or cell to maintain internal equilibrium by adjusting its physiological processes.

Intervention - Interference so as to modify a process or situation.

Intimacy - The state of being intimate; close familiarity or association; nearness in friendship.

Motivation - a motivating force, stimulus, or influence

Obsessive-compulsive behavior – repetitive, persistent ideas, thoughts, images, or impulses that are not experienced as subject to the will but intrude unwanted into the consciousness

Post traumatic stress syndrome – A characteristic group of symptoms triggered by an environmental event that is a severe enough stressor to evoke significant distress in almost any individual exposed to it.

Rationalization - a defense mechanism by which your true motivation is concealed by explaining your actions and feelings in a way that is not threatening

Regression - Reversion to an earlier or less mature pattern of feeling or behavior.

Repression - The unconscious exclusion of painful impulses, desires, or fears from the conscious mind.

Shame - A painful emotion caused by a strong sense of guilt, embarrassment, unworthiness, or disgrace.

Social Learning Theory – An approach to human behavior and personality that focuses on observable behaviors rather than postulating inner dynamics and drives and views behavior from the perspective of the actor rather than the observer.

Suppression - Conscious exclusion of unacceptable desires, thoughts, or memories from the mind.

Triangulation – In the context of family therapy a triangle consists of three people stuck in repetitious, maladaptive patterns of interaction.

Twelve Step Recovery Programs – Of or being a program designed to assist in the recovery from addiction or compulsive behavior, especially a spiritually-oriented program based on the principles of acknowledging one's personal insufficiency and accepting help from a higher power.

Victimizer - a person who victimizes others

Victims - One who is harmed by or made to suffer from an act, circumstance, agency, or condition

Withdrawal - Discontinuation of the use of an addictive substance

Bibliography

Annis, H. M. & Davis, C. S. (1991). *Alcohol, Health, and Research World,* pps. 204-212.

Carroll, Kathleen M., Ph.D. *A Cognitive-Behavioral Approach: Treating Cocaine Addiction.* National Institute on Drug Abuse (1998).

Chappel & Veach. *Resource Manual On Substance Abuse.* (1985). *Harvard Mental Health Letter.* (1992). pgs. 1-4.

DeKoven, Stan, Ph.D. *Assessment of Human Need.* Vision Publishing, Ramona, CA (1996).

DeKoven, Stan, Ph.D. *I Want to be Like You, Dad.* Vision Publishing, Ramona, CA (1996).

DeKoven, Stan, Ph.D. *Twelve Steps to Wholeness.* Vision Publishing, Ramona, CA (1996).

McCrady. B. S. (1991). *Alcohol, Health, and Research World,* pgs. 215-218.

McLellan, A. T., Childress, A. R., Griffith, J., & Woody, G. E. (1984). *American Journal of Drug and Alcohol Abuse,* pgs. 77-95.

Narramore, Bruce. *Model of Psychopathology developed from lecture,* 1982.

National Institute on Drug Abuse. *The Economic Costs of Alcohol and Drug Abuse in the United States.* (1992).

National Institute on Drug Abuse. *The Brain & the Actions of Cocaine, Opiates, and Marijuana.* (1998).

Peele, S. (1985). *The Meaning of Addiction: Compulsive Experience and its interpretation.* Lexington, MA: D. C. Health.

Thombs, Dennis L., Ph.D. *Introduction to Addictive Behavior.* 72 Sprint Street, New York, NY (1994).

Woody, G. E., Mclellan, A. T., Alterman, A. A., & O'Brien, C. P. (1991). *Alcohol, Health, and Research World,* pgs. 221-227.

Dennis L. Thombs Ph.D., (1994). *Introduction to Addictive Behavior.* 72 Sprint Street, New York, NY

Printed in the United States
61364LVS00005B/274-294